THIS IS MY FIRST TIME SO PLEASE BE BRUTAL

Vincent Truman

THIS IS MY FIRST TIME SO PLEASE BE BRUTAL
by Vincent Truman
First Edition

ISBN: 978-1-4357-0685-9

Printed in the United States of America
or someplace else with cheap labor.

http: // www.vincenttruman.net
http://www.suspiciousclowns.net

for Jennifer

INTRODUCTION
by Vincent Truman

I can't really draw. Sorry.

In the earliest drawings I can find, dating back to when I was three or four, I can see I was highly advanced for my age. My notebooks did not have stick figures or poorly executed drawings that did not make an accurate leap from my imagination to the page; rather, all characters had full bodies, correct numbers of fingers and even logical, if childlike, narratives that one could follow. While my contemporaries were attempting to stay in the lines while coloring, my kindergarten teacher praised my work, and held it aloft in class to show the other students what they *should* be doing. It is obvious while looking at these illustrations that I was destined to become a fantastic artist.

And then it stopped. I do not know when, how or why my development ceased, but I reached a peak in first or second grade and never improved. I tried from time to time to evolve to the next artistic level, but it was as fruitful as a paraplegic picking avocados. Thus, the cartoons you see in these pages are very much like the ones my seven-year-old self would doodle endlessly on the front porch of my family's home.

However, one thing that did develop, and continues to develop, is a rather acerbic sense of humor. Borne out of taking reality to its logical conclusion coupled with a love of bad puns, my sense of humor often strikes people as twisted at best and very twisted at worst. Despite this, I have entertained quite a few friends with it through the years, either through my improvisational comedy work or my tenure with the sketch comedy group called Suspicious Clowns.

This book is a fusion of these two passions of mine, one of which is horribly underdeveloped. I hope you like it – or cringe, which is just 'like' with a lemon.

Best,

Vincent Truman
January 2008

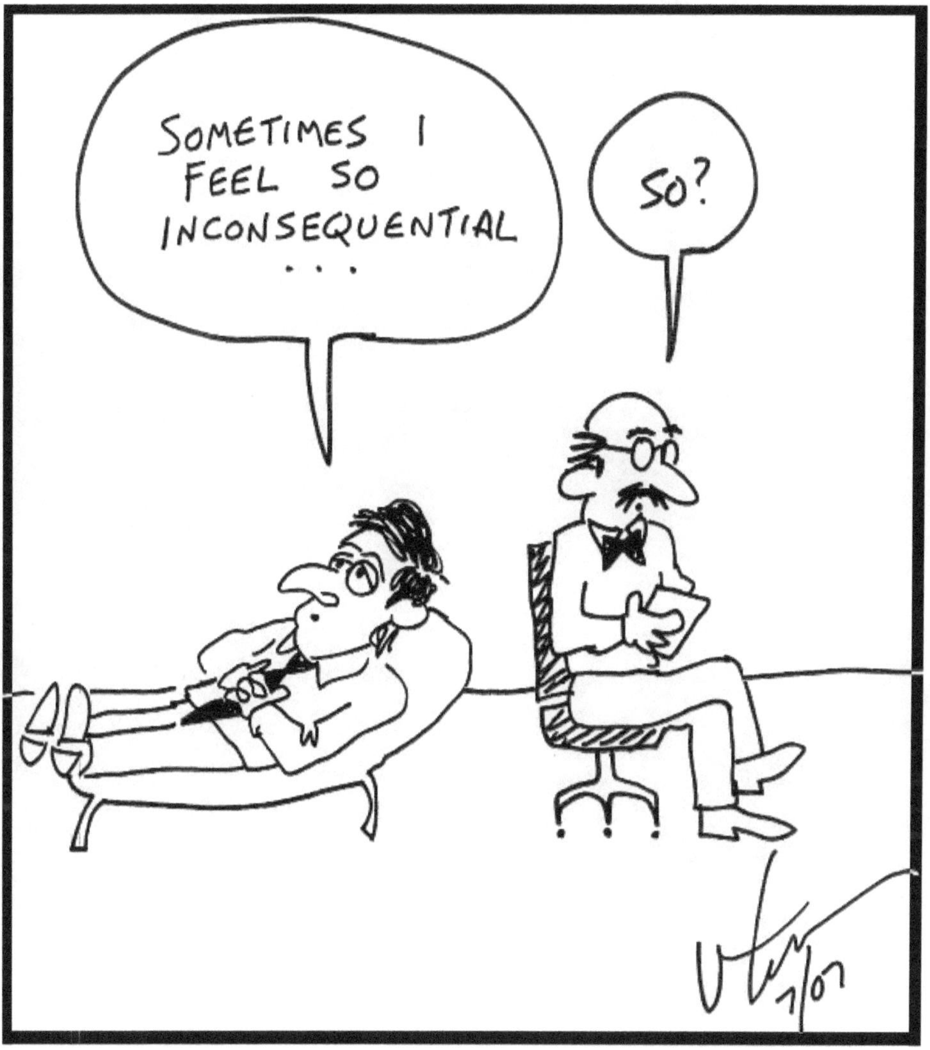
SOMETIMES I FEEL SO INCONSEQUENTIAL . . .
SO?

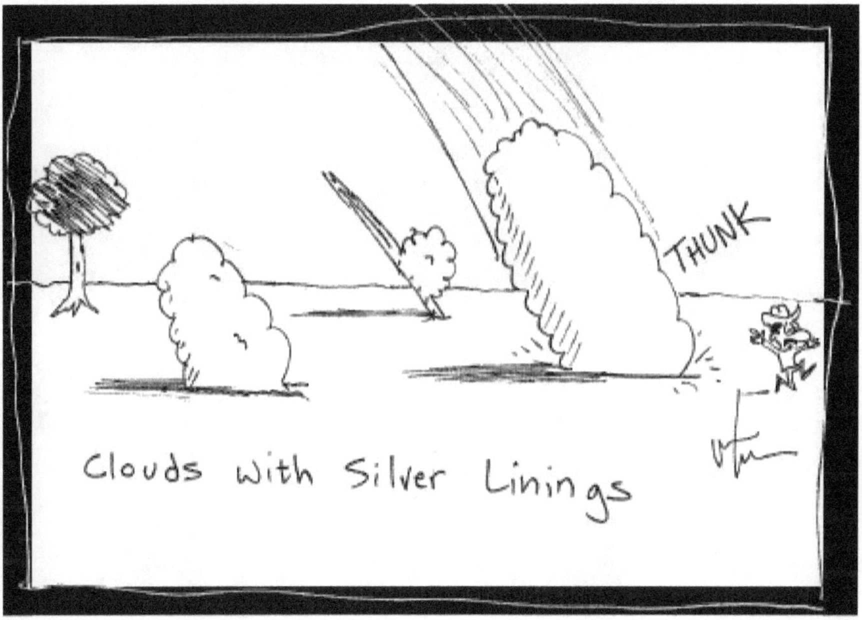
THUNK
Clouds with Silver Linings

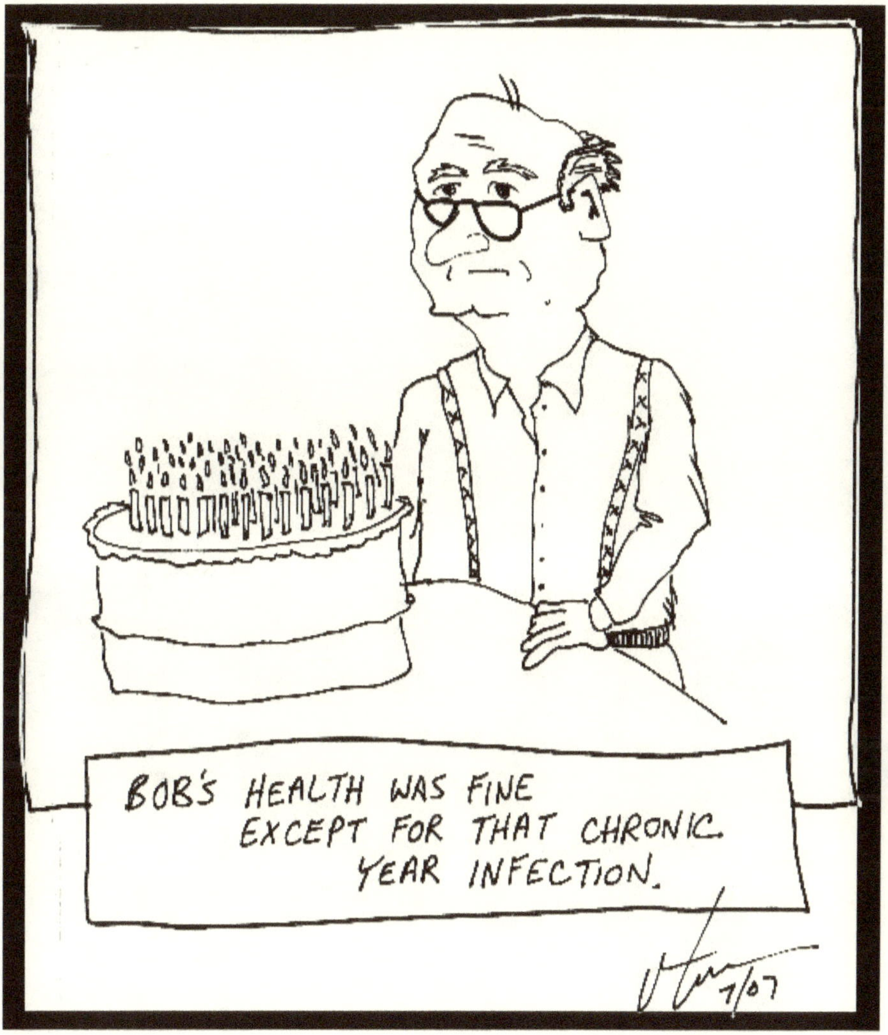
BOB'S HEALTH WAS FINE
EXCEPT FOR THAT CHRONIC
YEAR INFECTION.
7/07

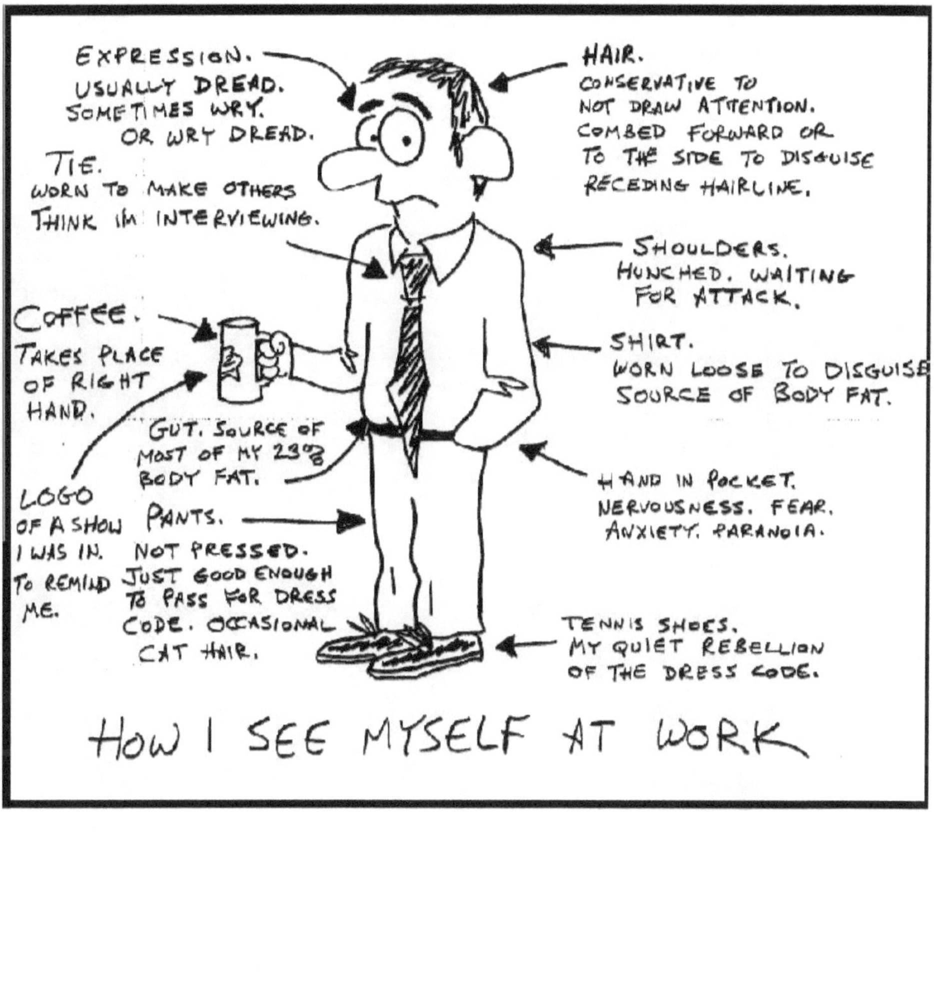
EXPRESSION. USUALLY DREAD. SOMETIMES WRY. OR WRY DREAD.
HAIR. CONSERVATIVE TO NOT DRAW ATTENTION. COMBED FORWARD OR TO THE SIDE TO DISGUISE RECEDING HAIRLINE.
TIE. WORN TO MAKE OTHERS THINK IM INTERVIEWING.
SHOULDERS. HUNCHED. WAITING FOR ATTACK.
COFFEE. TAKES PLACE OF RIGHT HAND.
SHIRT. WORN LOOSE TO DISGUISE SOURCE OF BODY FAT.
GUT. SOURCE OF MOST OF MY 23% BODY FAT.
HAND IN POCKET. NERVOUSNESS. FEAR. ANXIETY. PARANOIA.
LOGO OF A SHOW I WAS IN. TO REMIND ME.
PANTS. NOT PRESSED. JUST GOOD ENOUGH TO PASS FOR DRESS CODE. OCCASIONAL CAT HAIR.
TENNIS SHOES. MY QUIET REBELLION OF THE DRESS CODE.
HOW I SEE MYSELF AT WORK

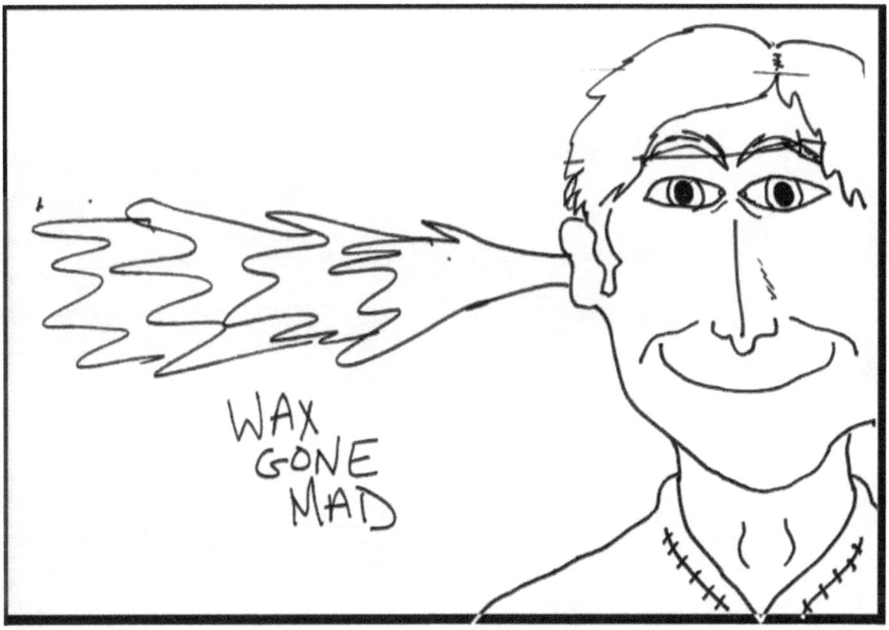
WAX
GONE
MAD

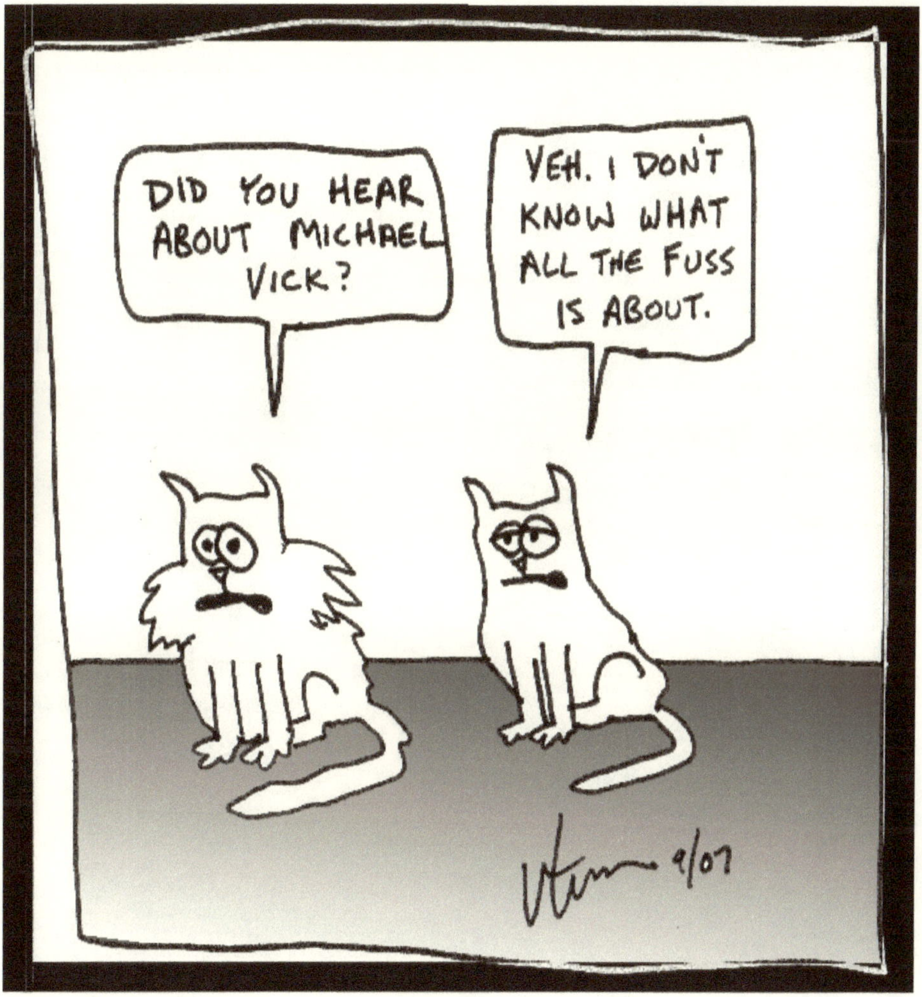
DID YOU HEAR ABOUT MICHAEL VICK?
YEH. I DON'T KNOW WHAT ALL THE FUSS IS ABOUT.

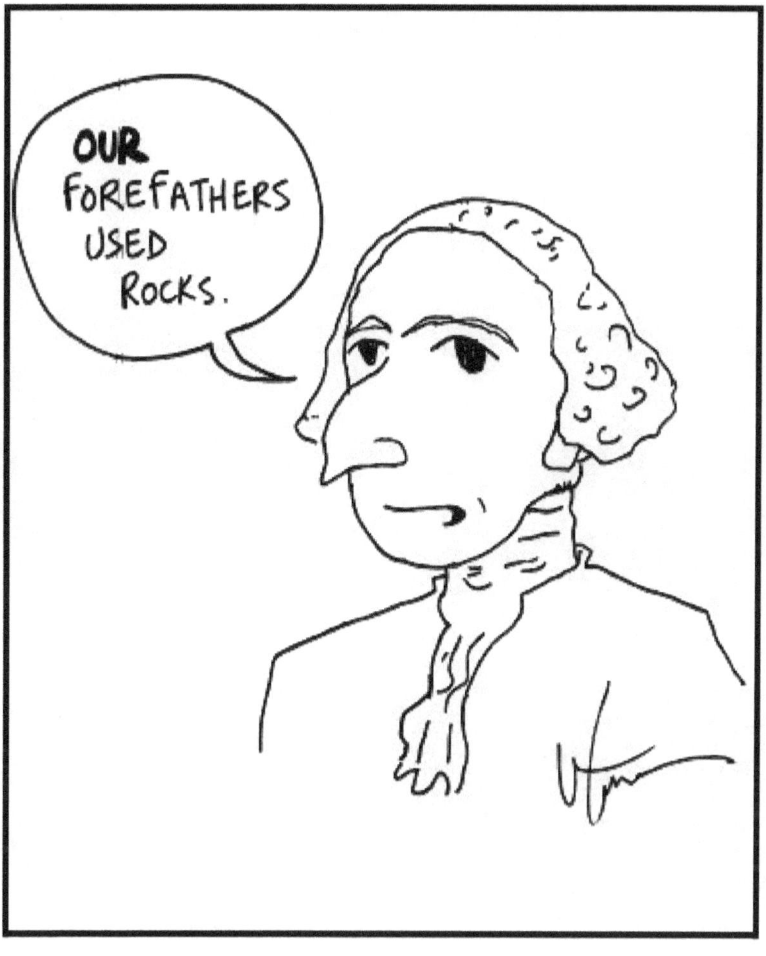
OUR FOREFATHERS USED ROCKS.

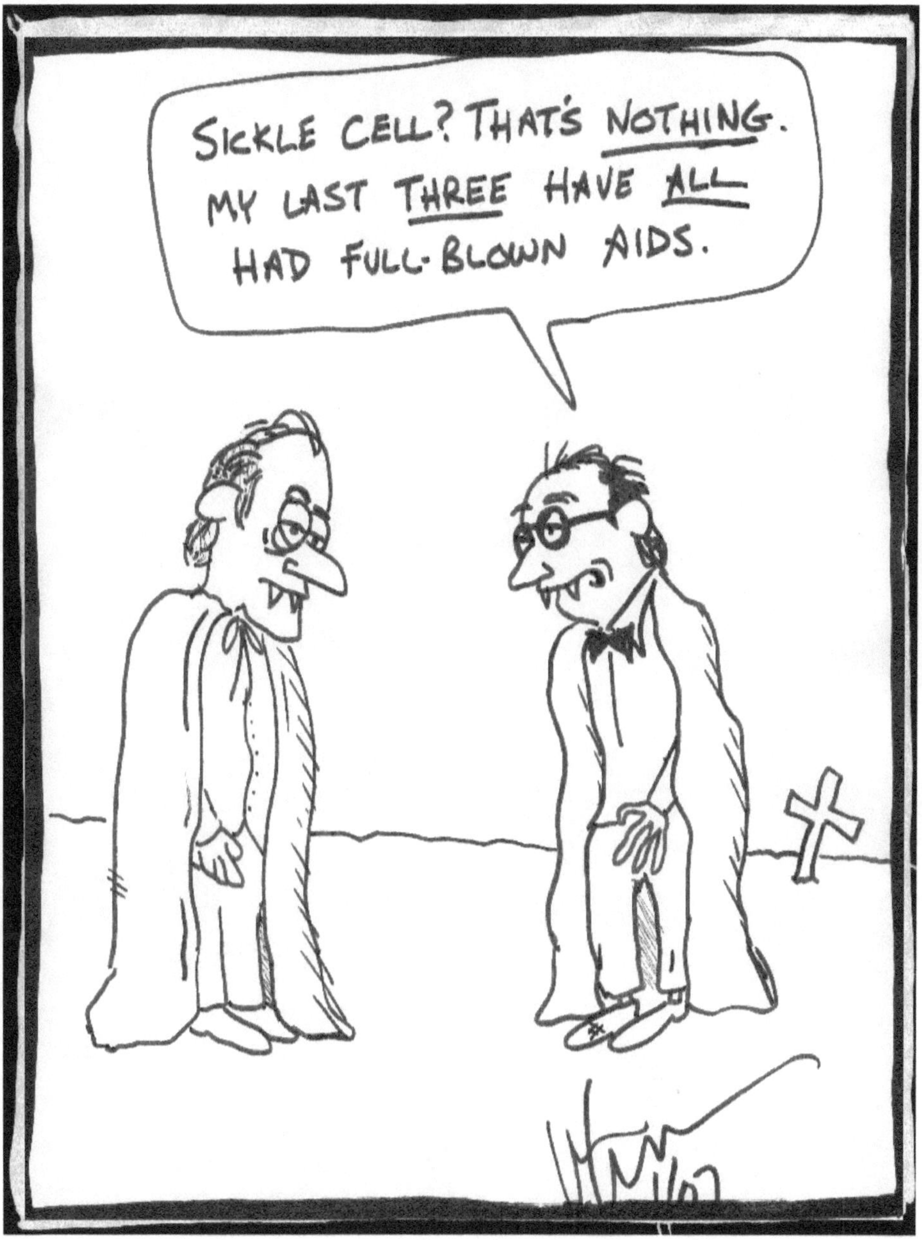
SICKLE CELL? THAT'S NOTHING. MY LAST THREE HAVE ALL HAD FULL-BLOWN AIDS.

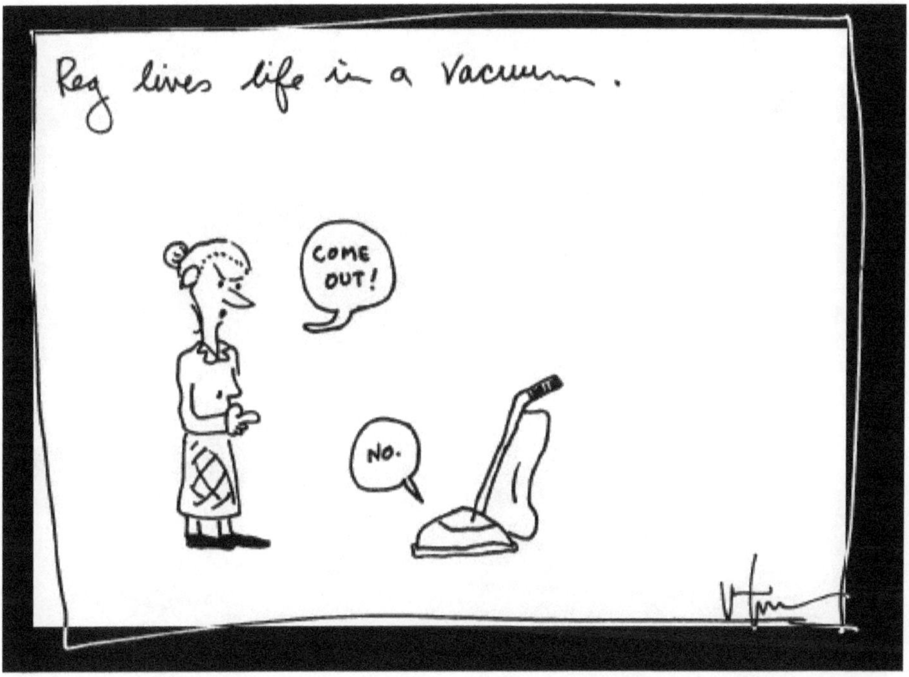
Reg lives life in a vacuum.
COME OUT!
NO.

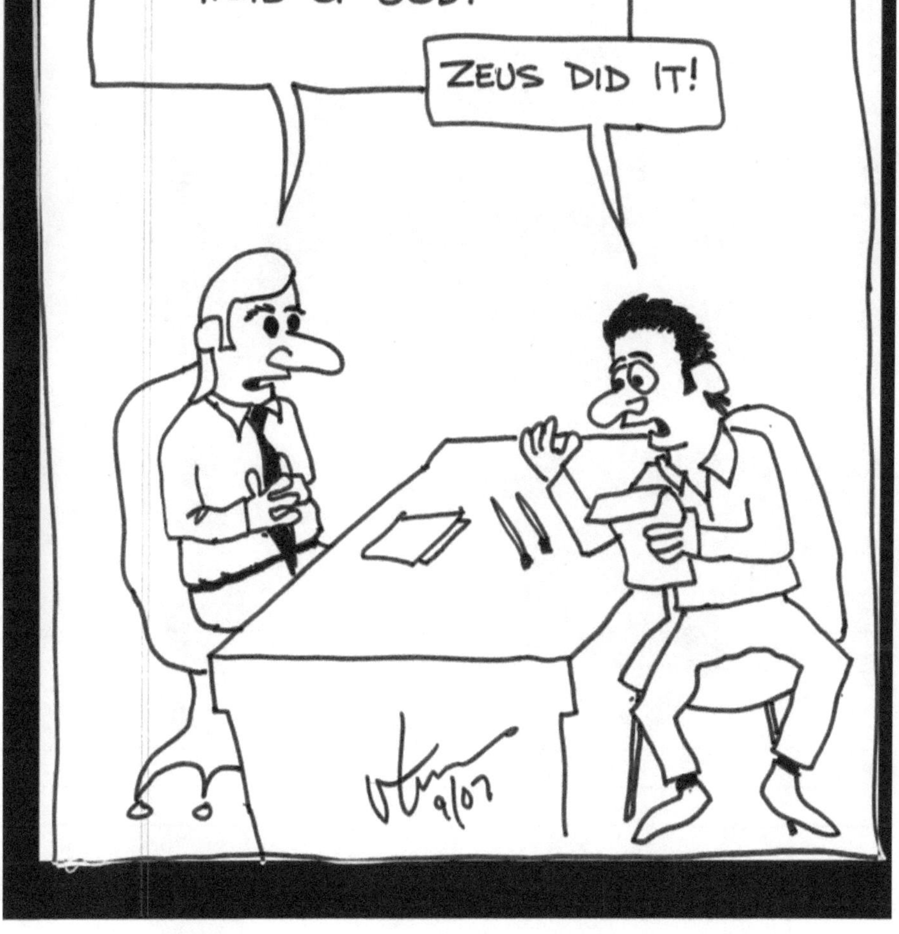
WE'RE SORRY YOUR HOUSE WAS DESTOYED, BUT WE DO NOT INSURE AGAINST ACTS OF GOD.
ZEUS DID IT!

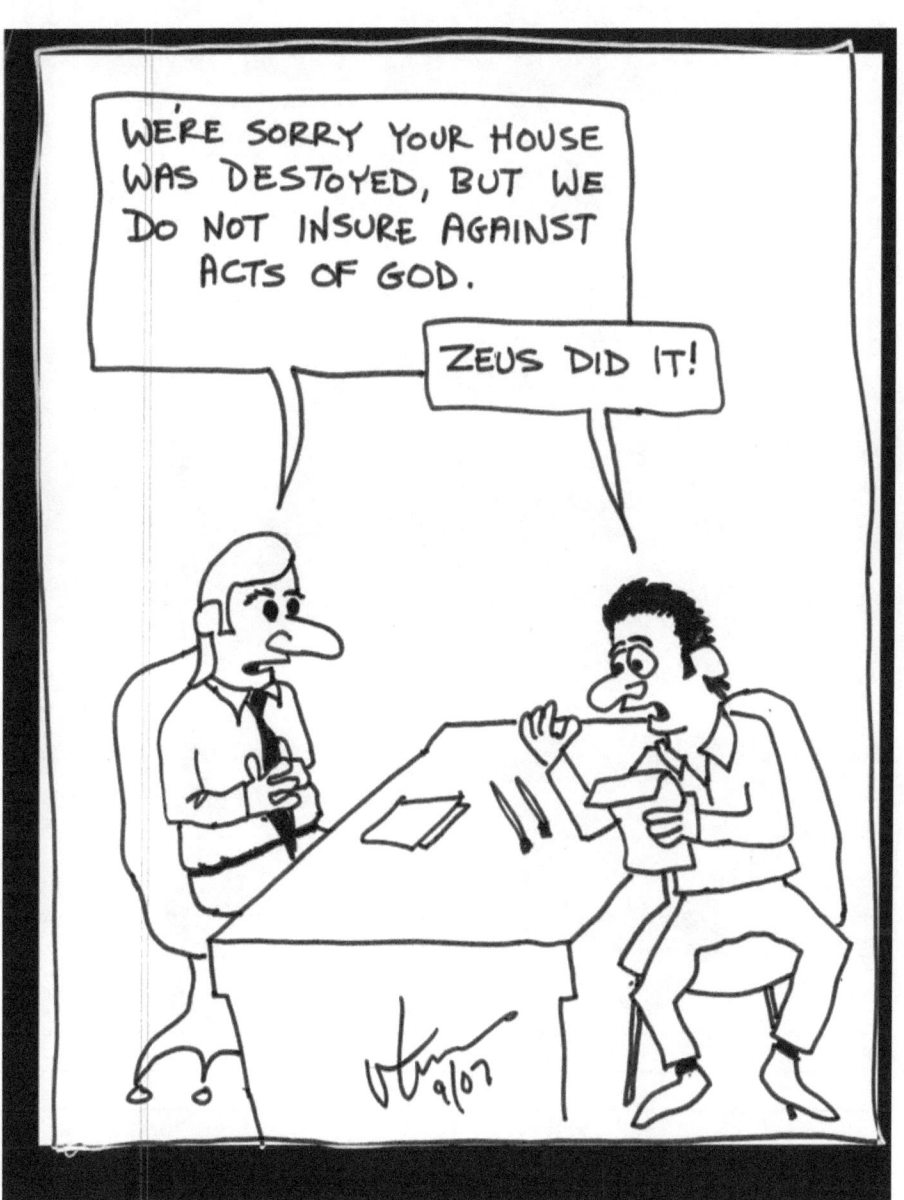

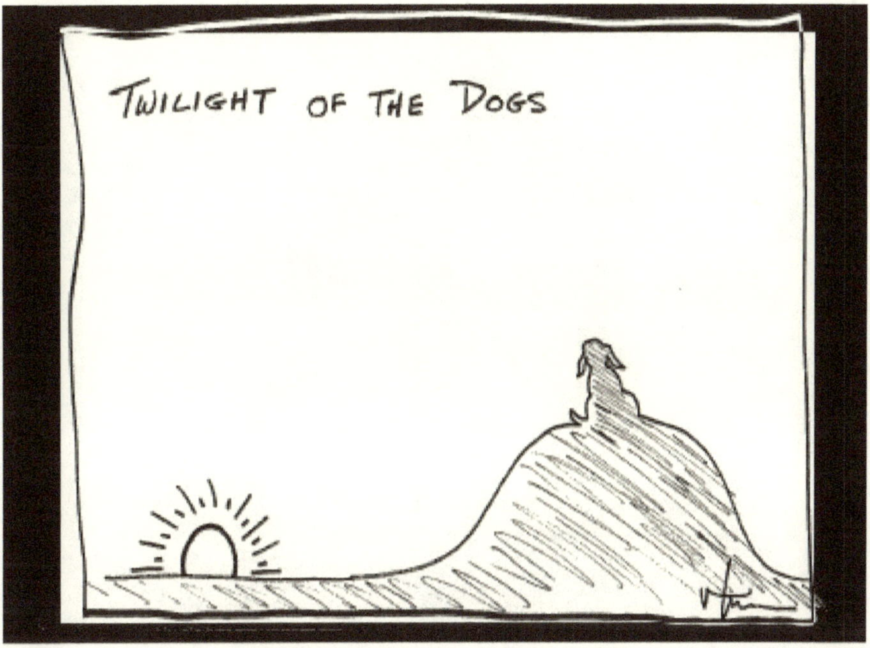
TWILIGHT OF THE DOGS

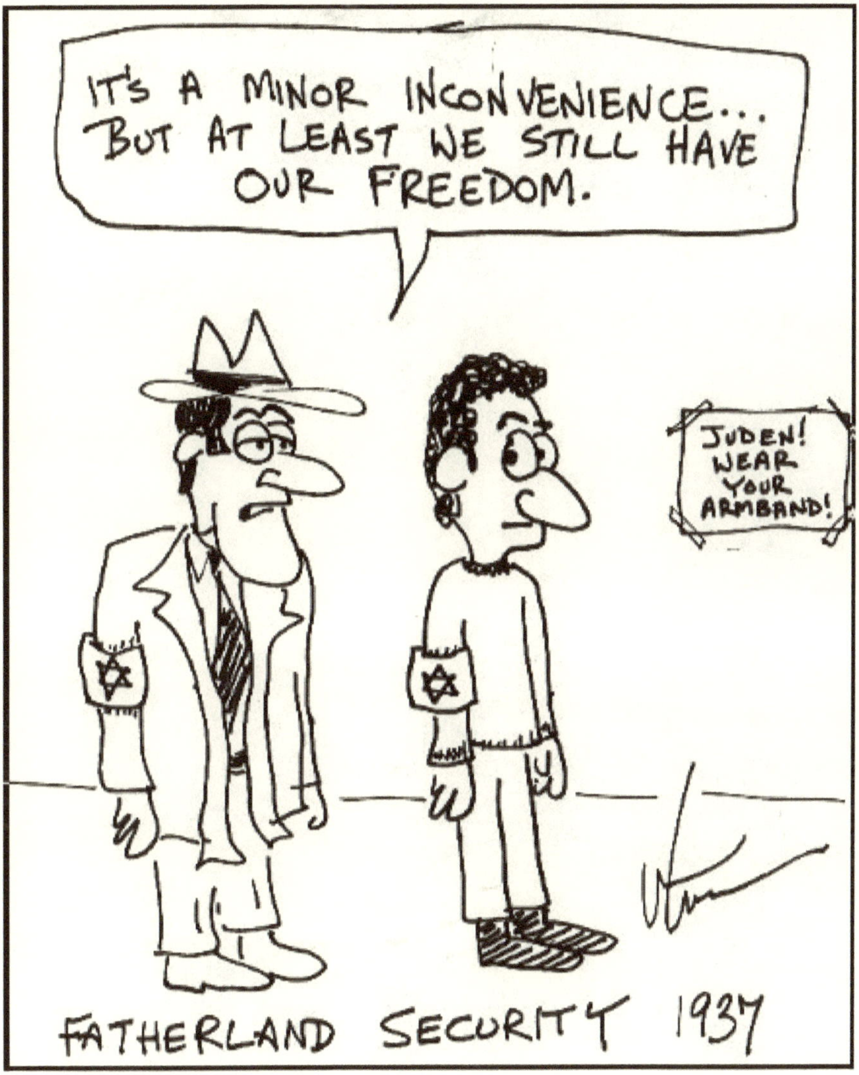
IT'S A MINOR INCONVENIENCE... BUT AT LEAST WE STILL HAVE OUR FREEDOM.
JUDEN! WEAR YOUR ARMBAND!
FATHERLAND SECURITY 1937

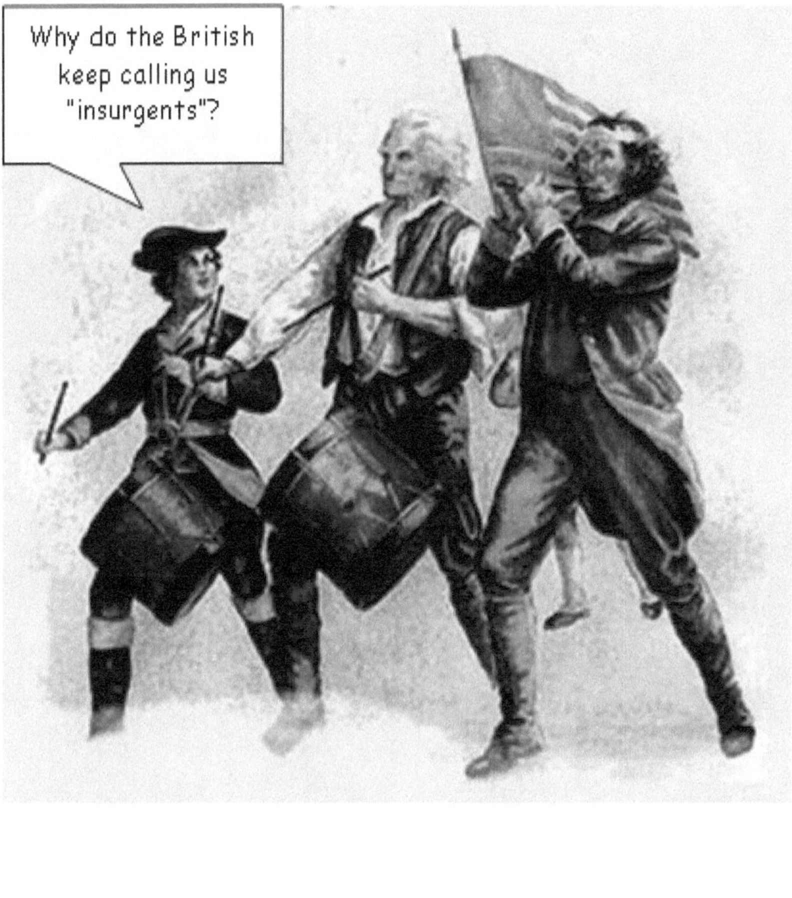
Why do the British keep calling us "insurgents"?

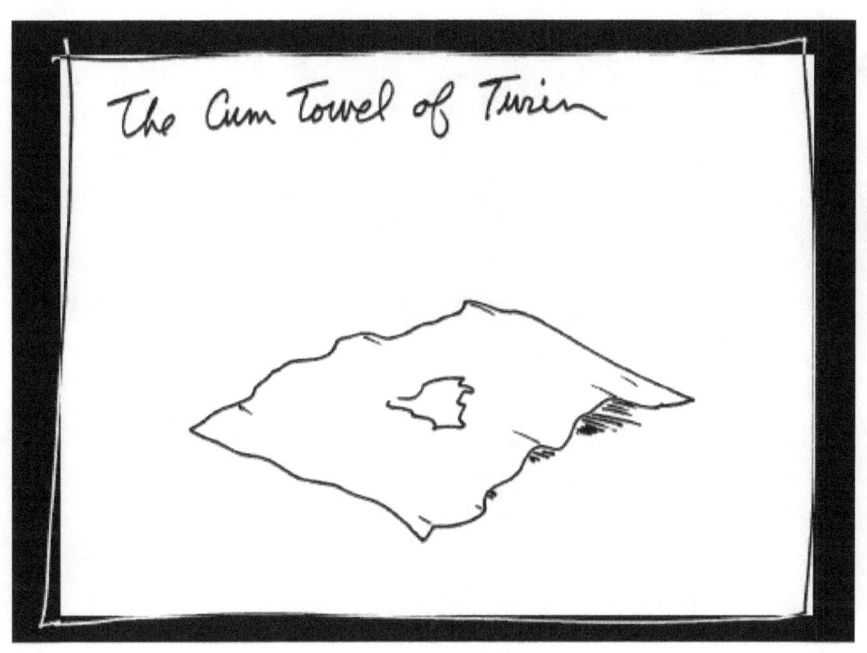

The Cum Towel of Turin

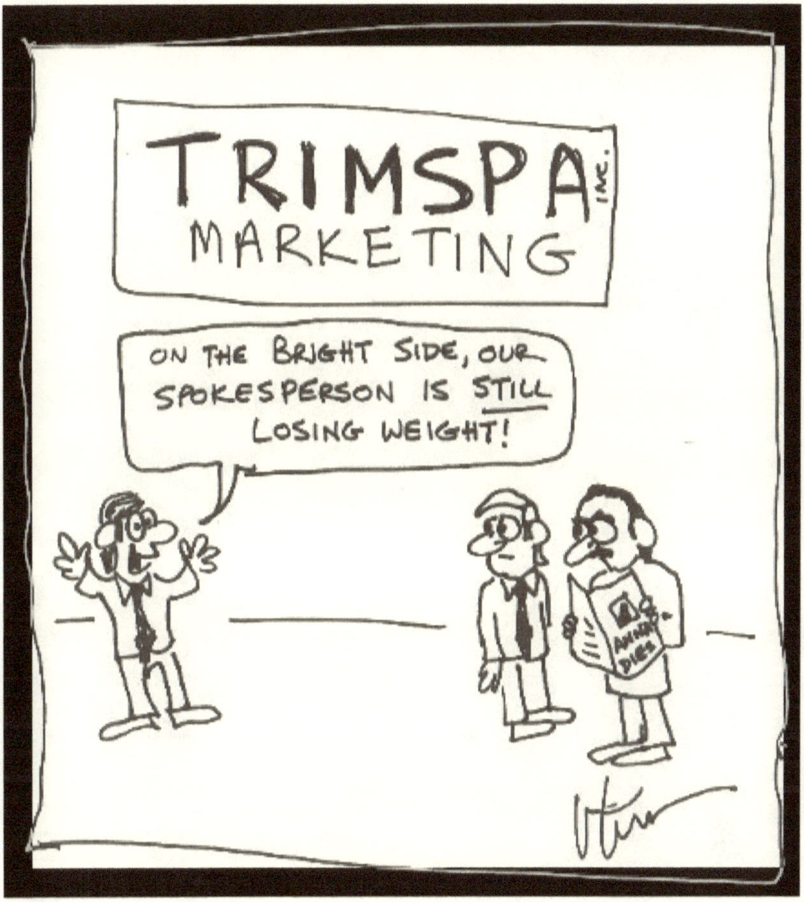
TRIMSPA INC.
MARKETING
ON THE BRIGHT SIDE, OUR SPOKESPERSON IS STILL LOSING WEIGHT!

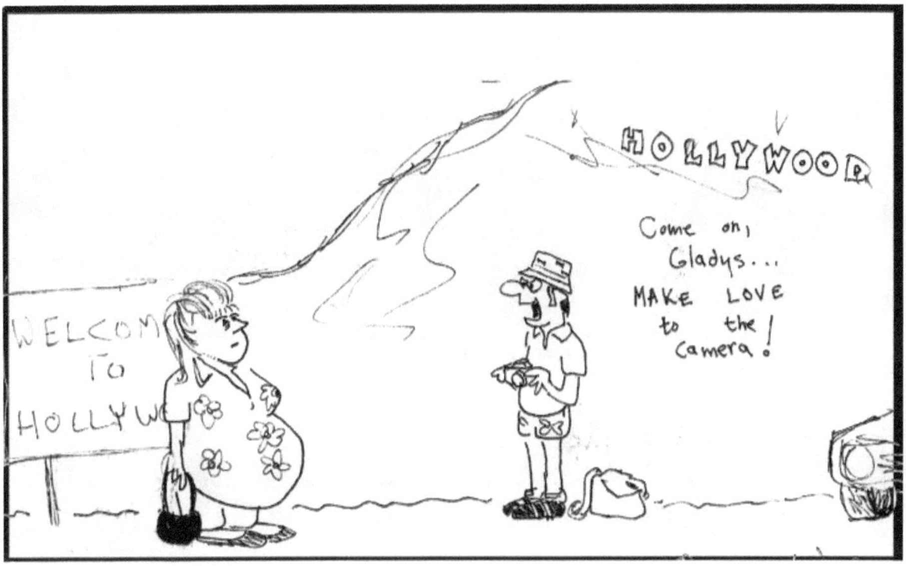
HOLLYWOOD
Come on, Gladys... MAKE LOVE to the camera!

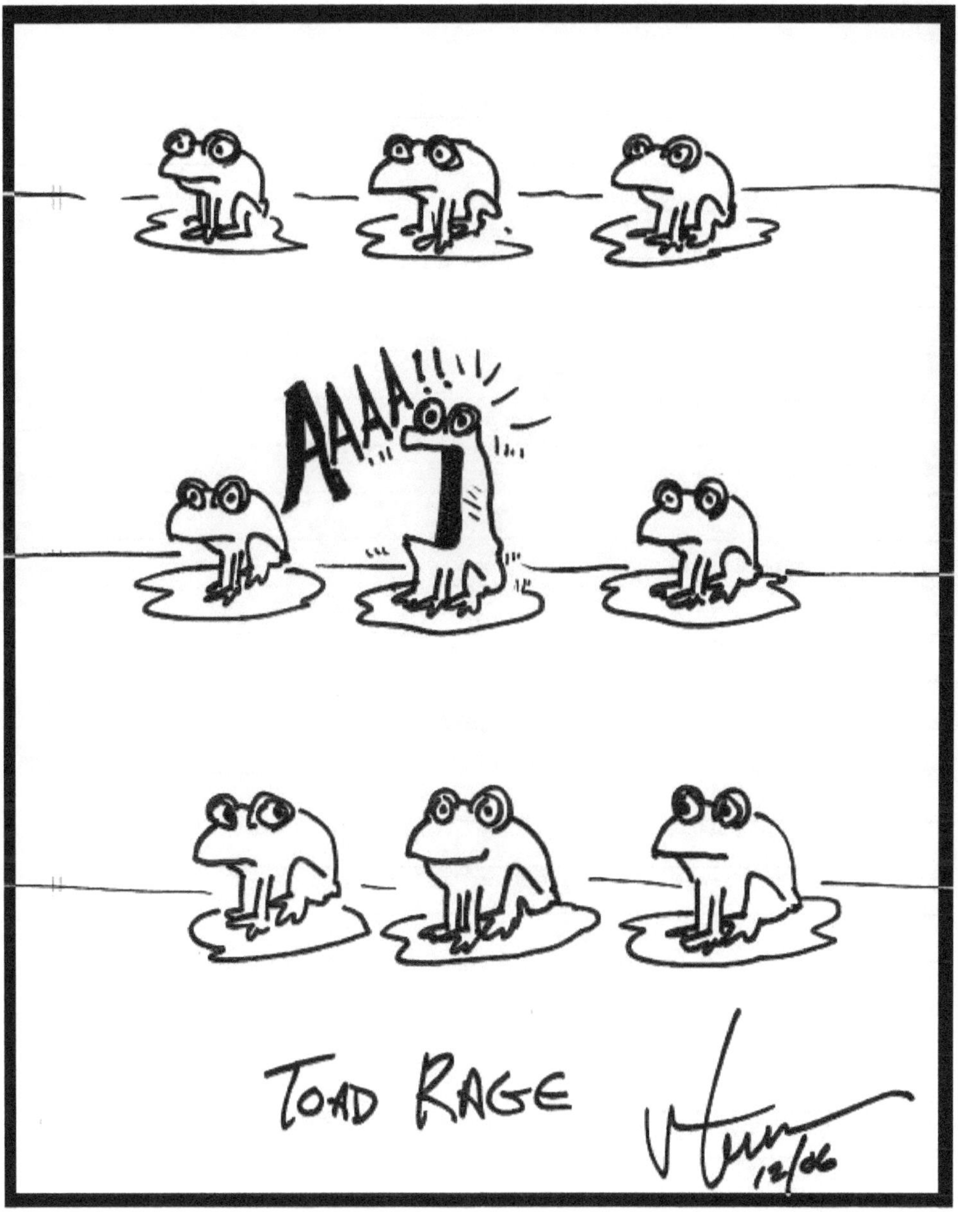
AAAA!!!
TOAD RAGE
12/06

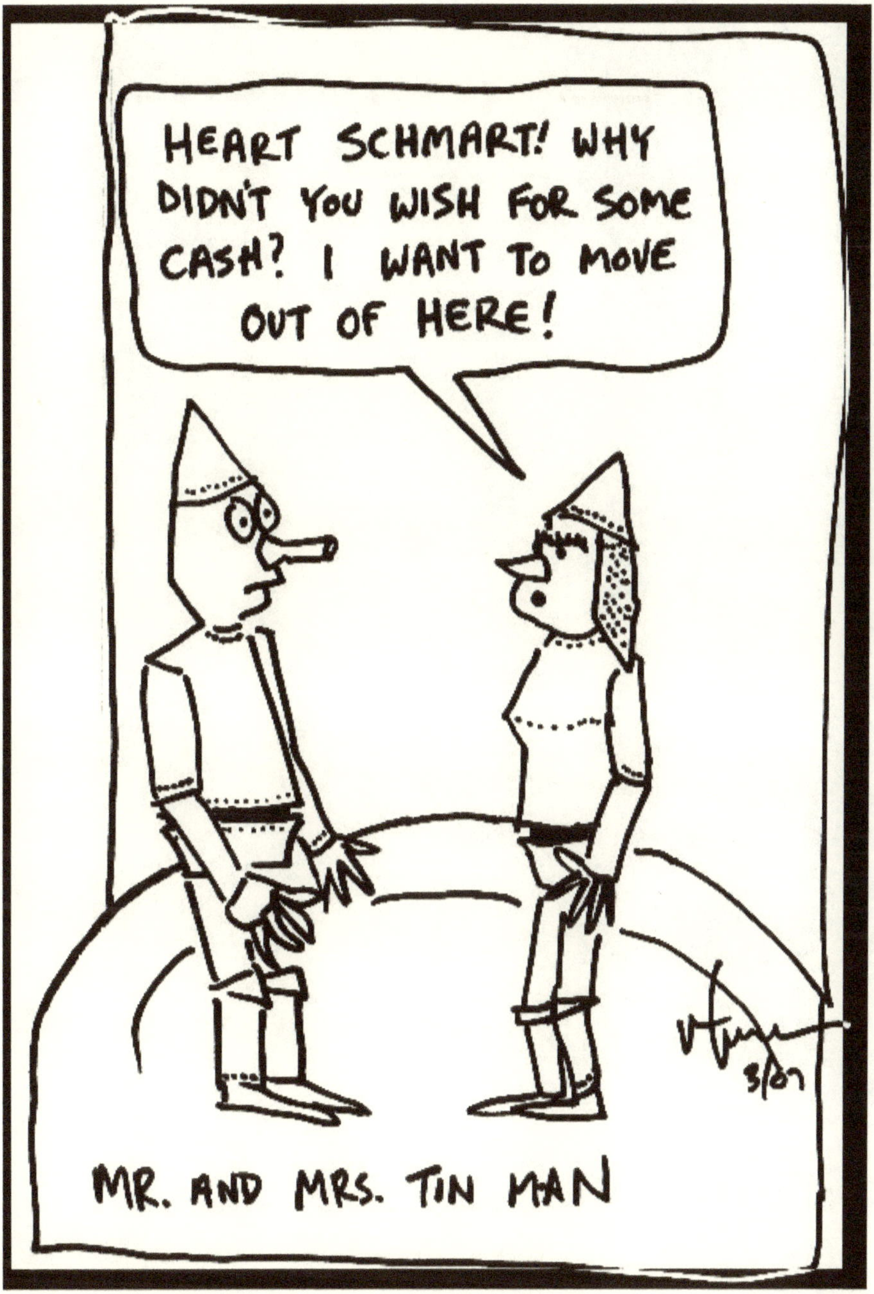
HEART SCHMART! WHY DIDN'T YOU WISH FOR SOME CASH? I WANT TO MOVE OUT OF HERE!
MR. AND MRS. TIN MAN

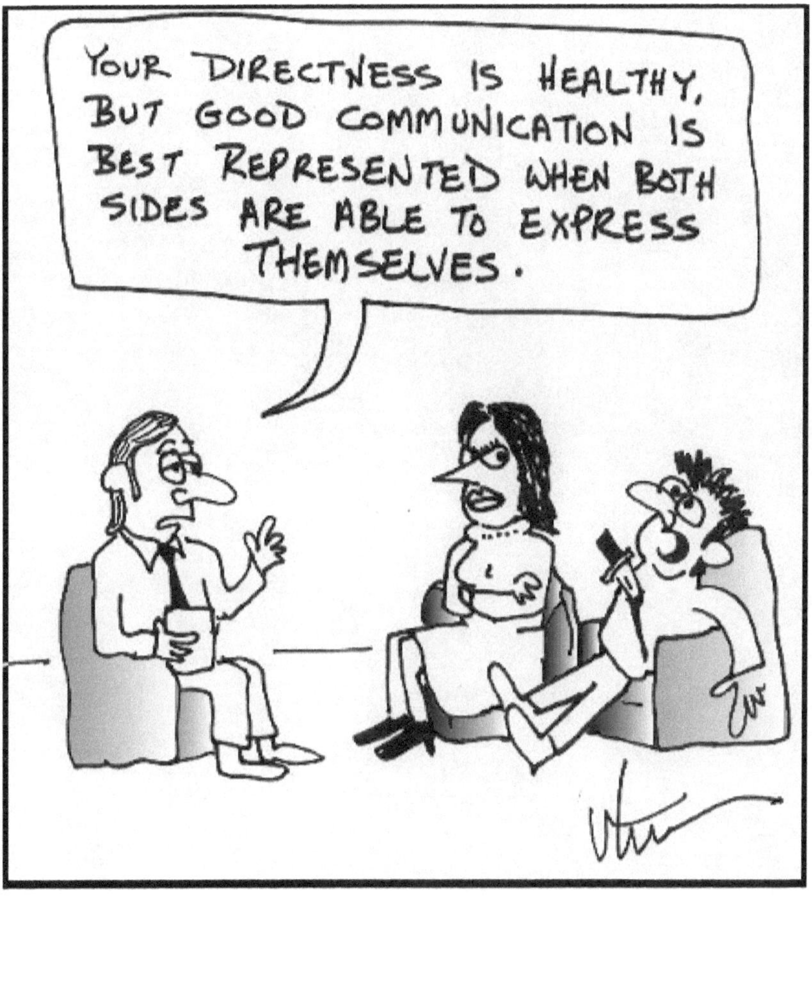
YOUR DIRECTNESS IS HEALTHY, BUT GOOD COMMUNICATION IS BEST REPRESENTED WHEN BOTH SIDES ARE ABLE TO EXPRESS THEMSELVES.

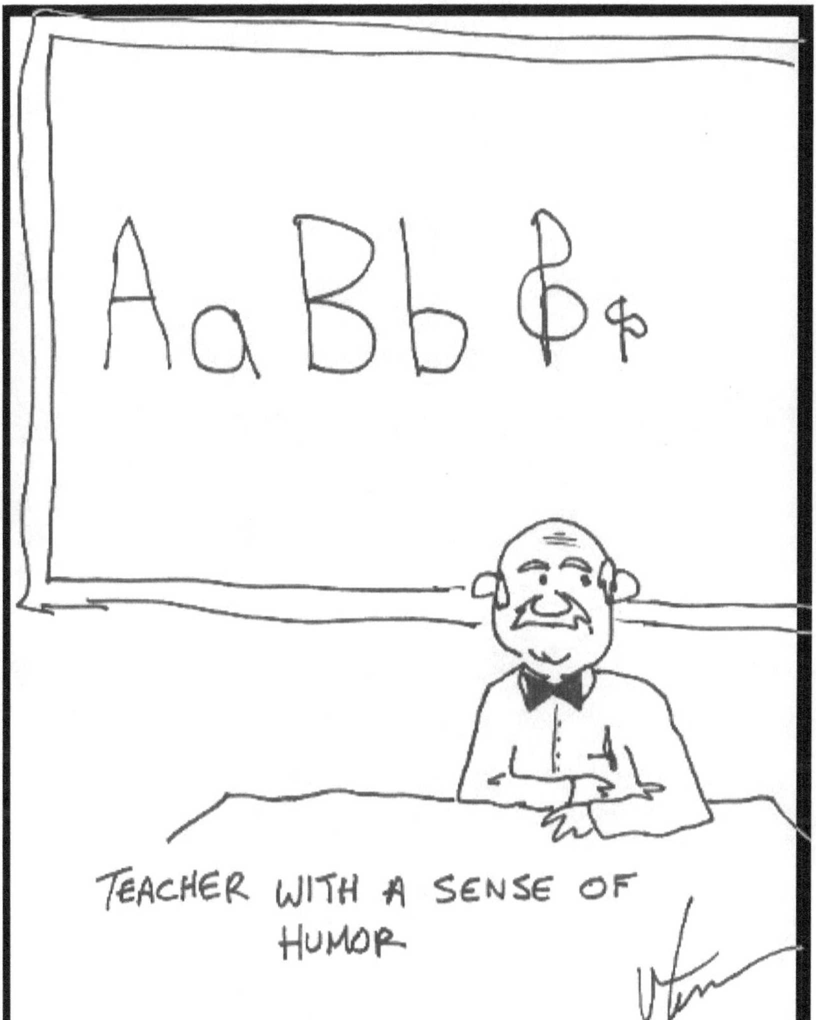
AaBb
TEACHER WITH A SENSE OF HUMOR

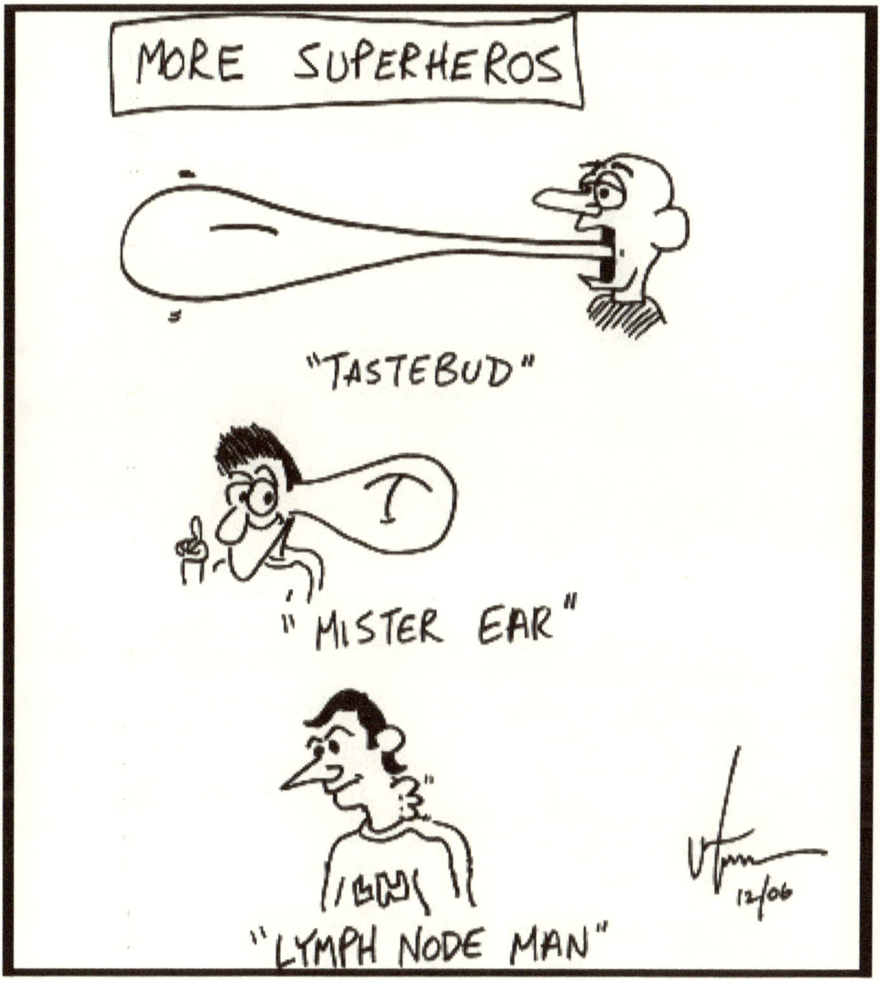
MORE SUPERHEROS
"TASTEBUD"
"MISTER EAR"
"LYMPH NODE MAN"
12/06

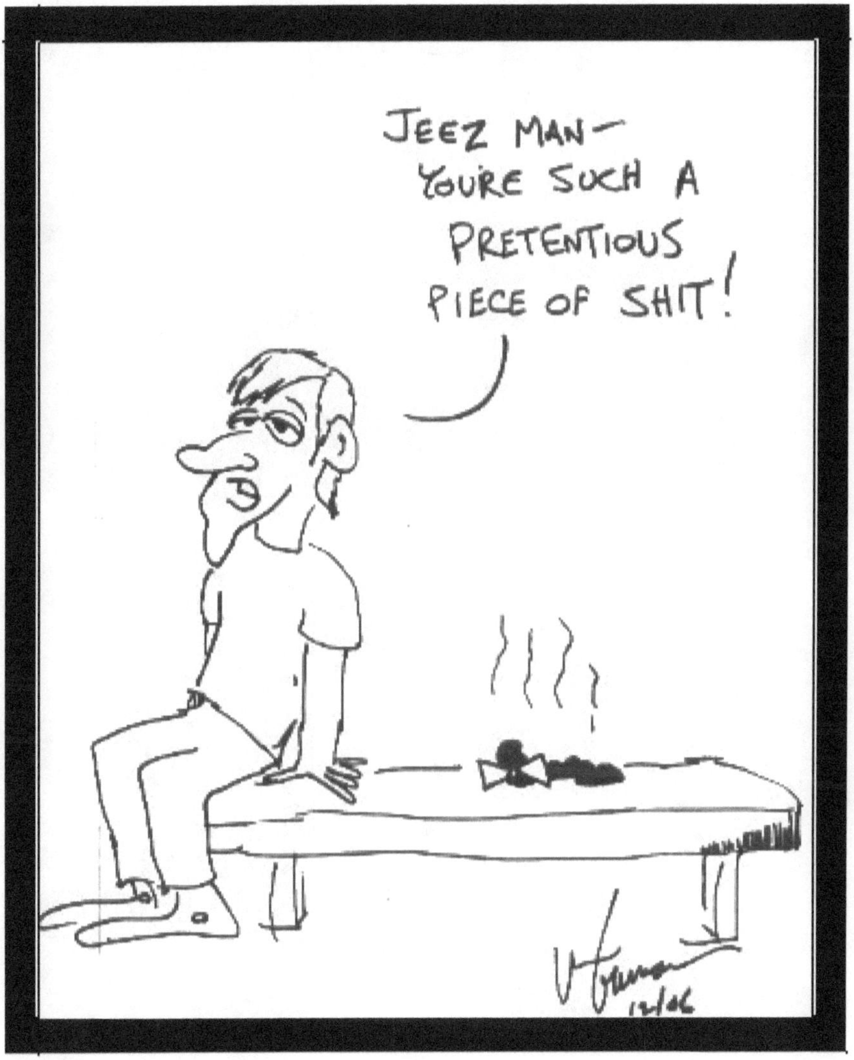
JEEZ MAN-
YOU'RE SUCH A
PRETENTIOUS
PIECE OF SHIT!

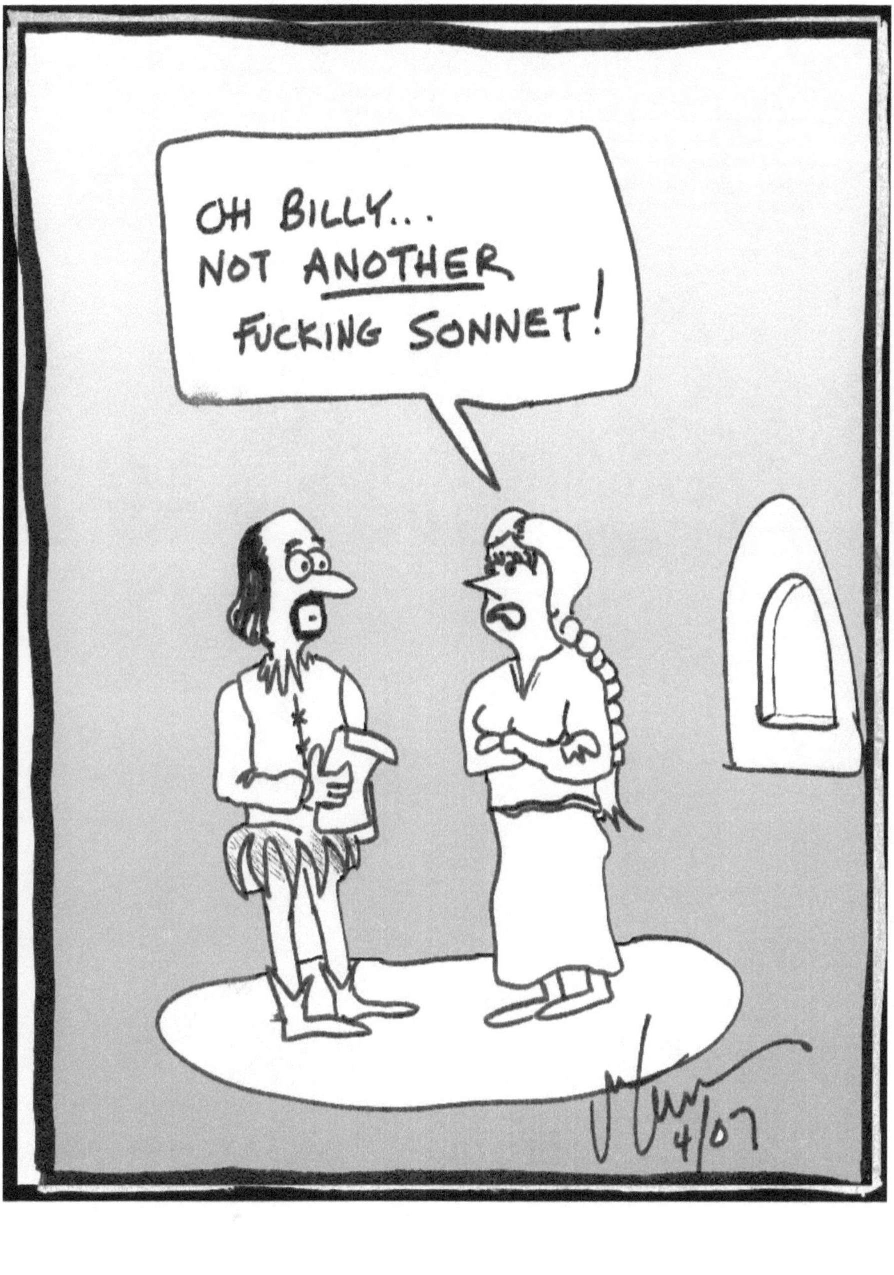
OH BILLY... NOT ANOTHER FUCKING SONNET!

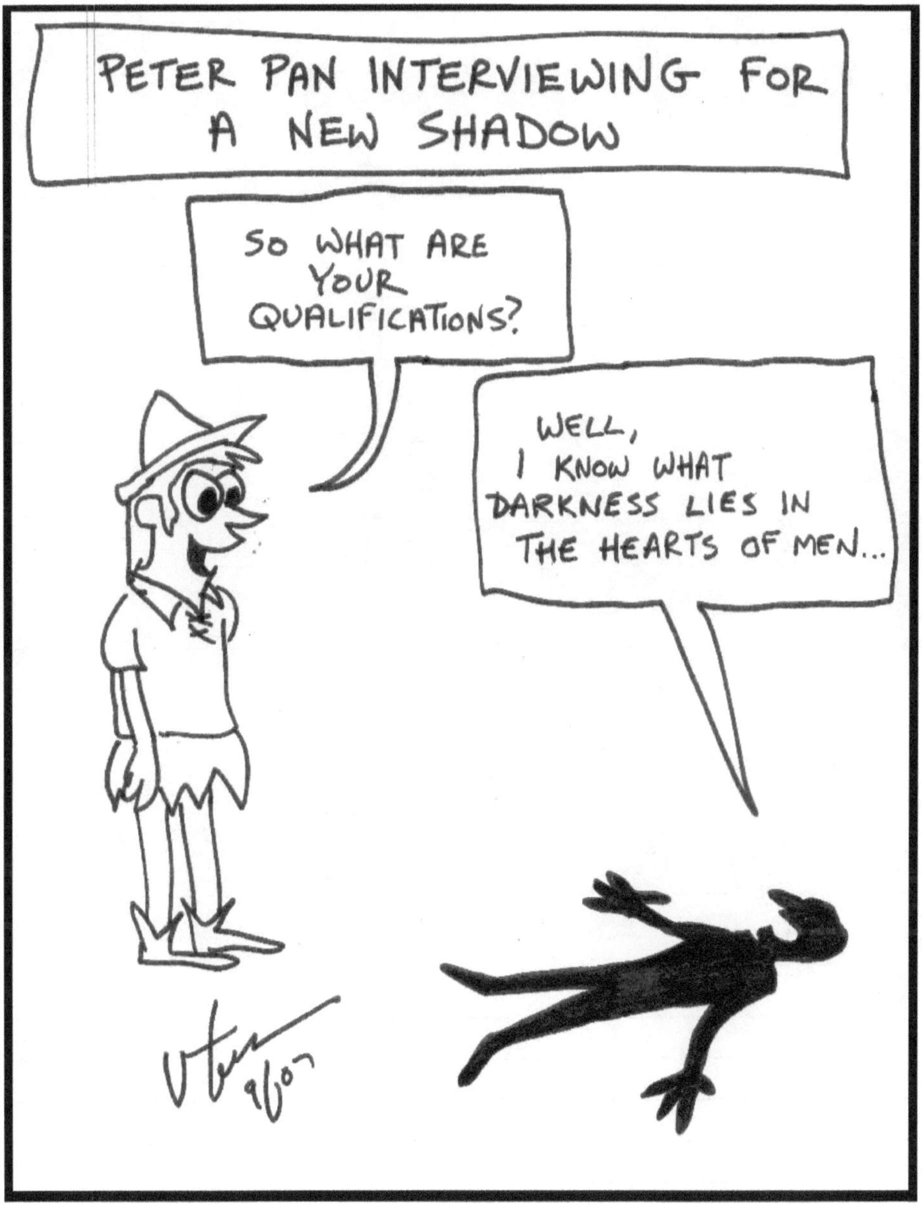
PETER PAN INTERVIEWING FOR A NEW SHADOW
SO WHAT ARE YOUR QUALIFICATIONS?
WELL, I KNOW WHAT DARKNESS LIES IN THE HEARTS OF MEN...

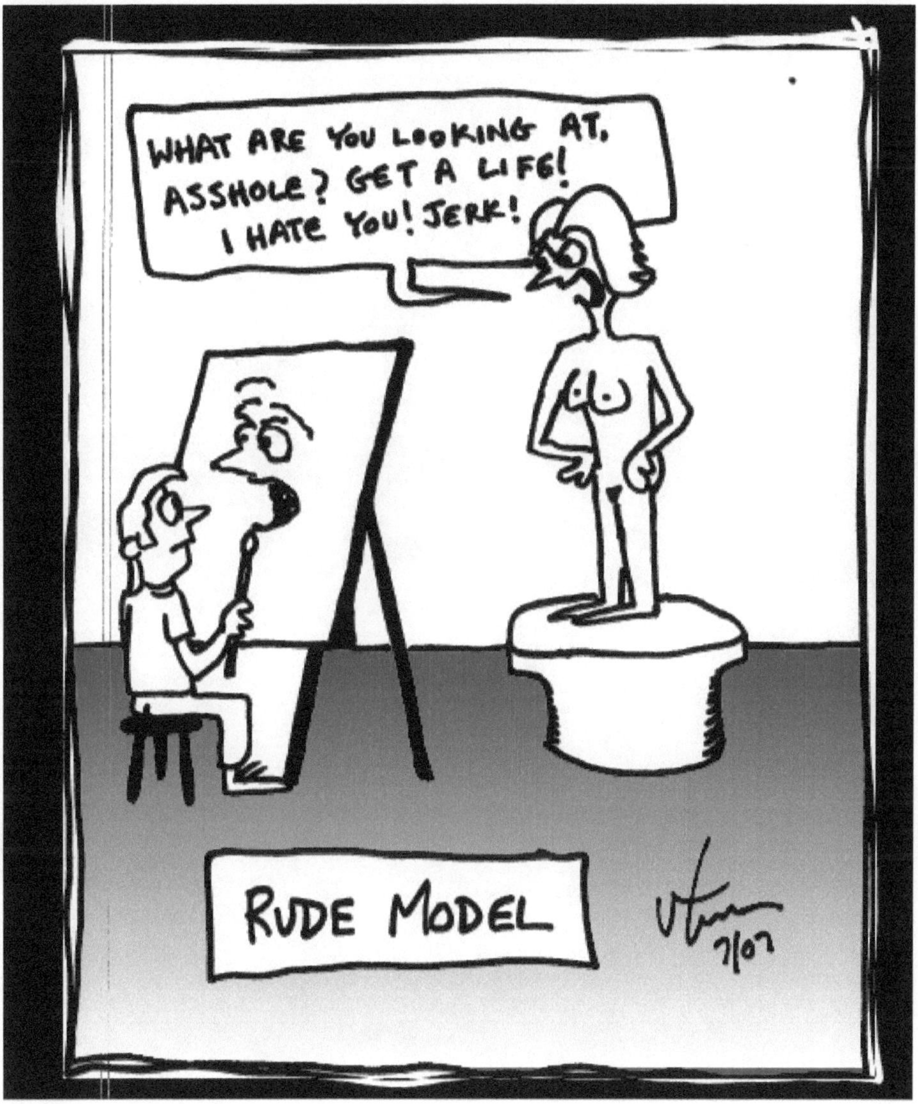
WHAT ARE YOU LOOKING AT, ASSHOLE? GET A LIFE! I HATE YOU! JERK!
RUDE MODEL

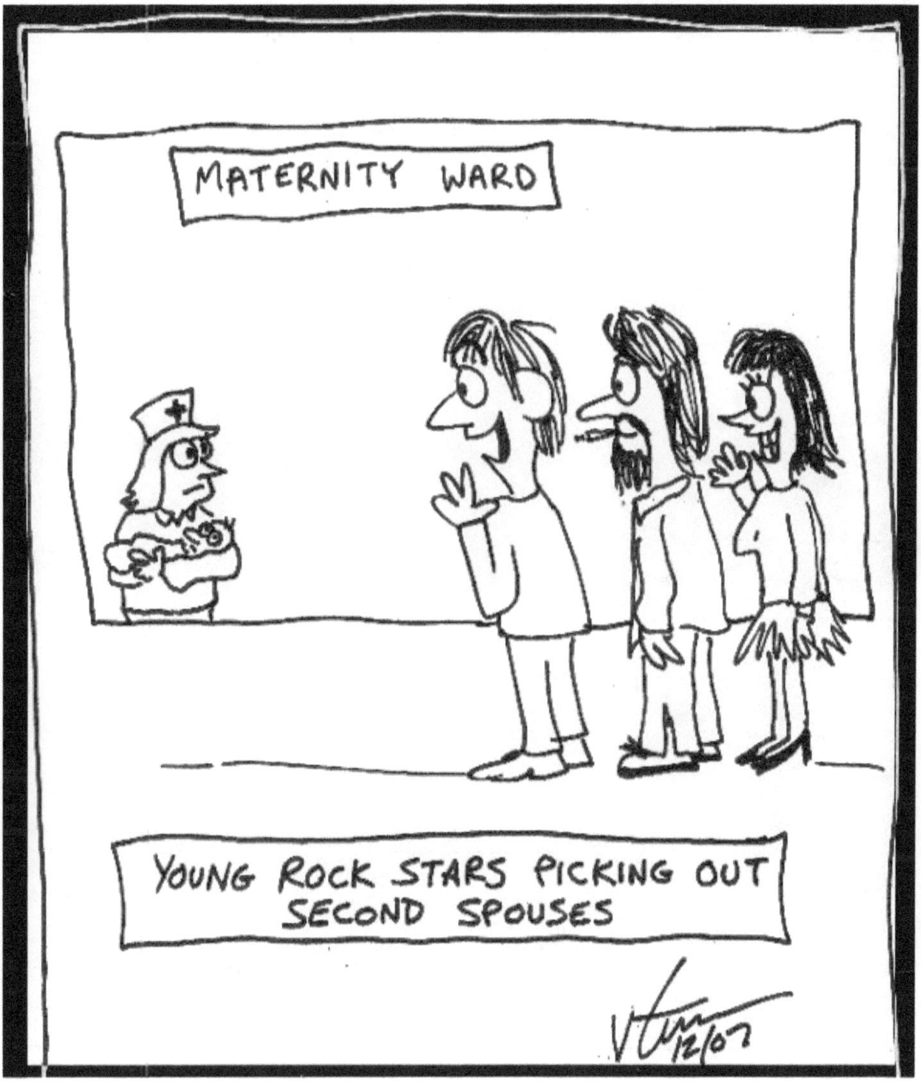
MATERNITY WARD
YOUNG ROCK STARS PICKING OUT SECOND SPOUSES
12/07

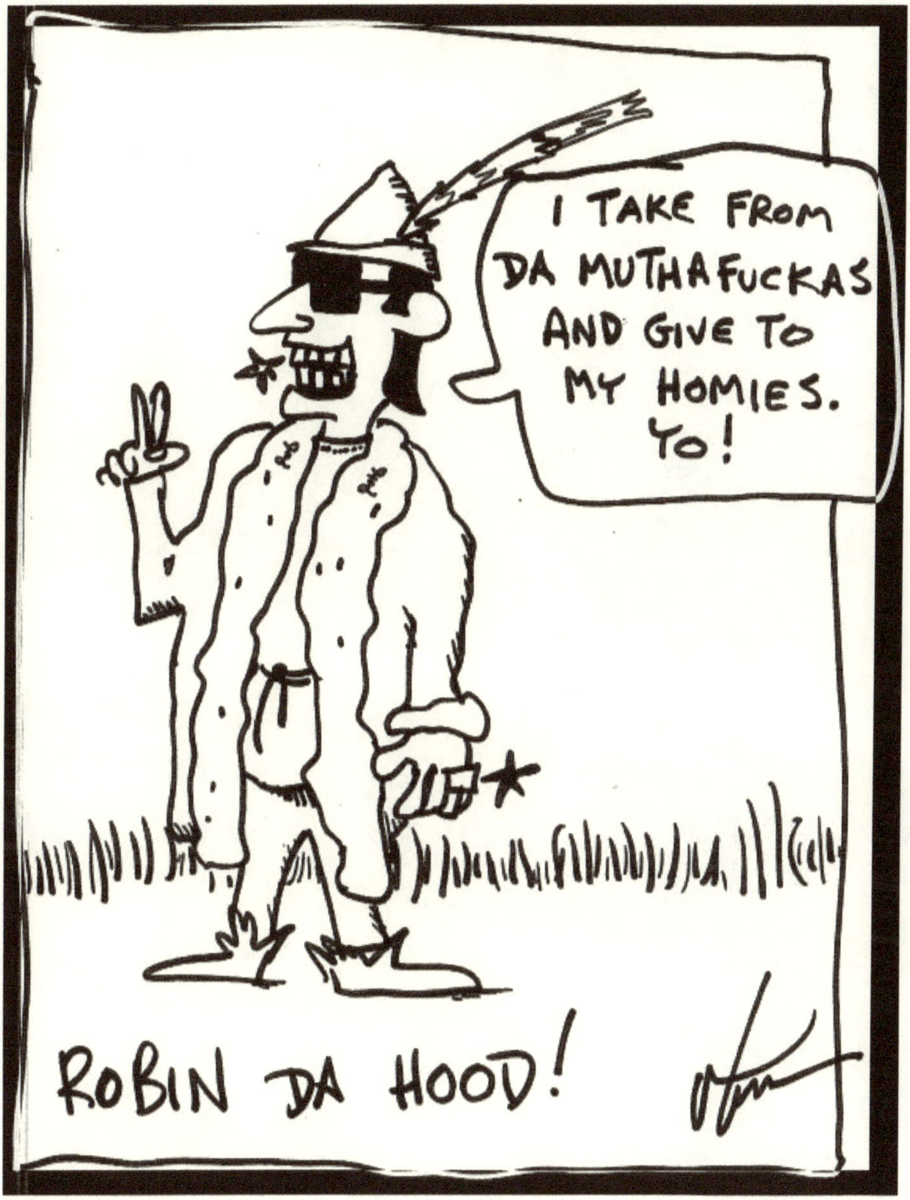
I TAKE FROM DA MUTHAFUCKAS AND GIVE TO MY HOMIES. YO!
ROBIN DA HOOD!

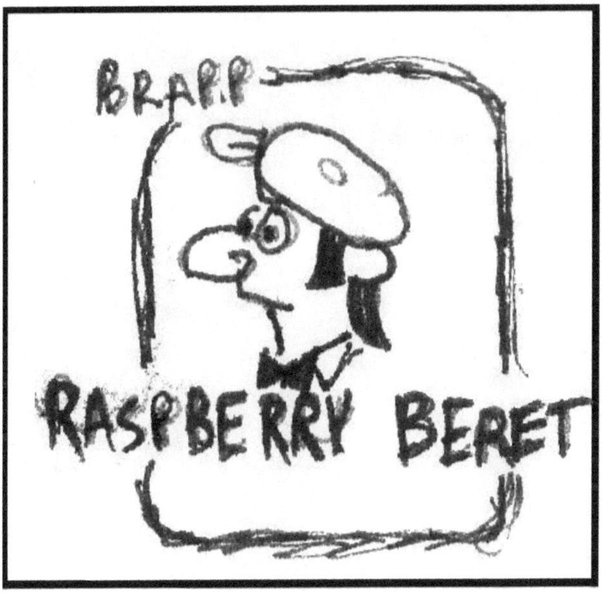
BRAPP
RASPBERRY BERET

THE ADVENTURES OF RACIST AIDS MONKEY!

based on an idea by Robert Felker & Vincent Truman

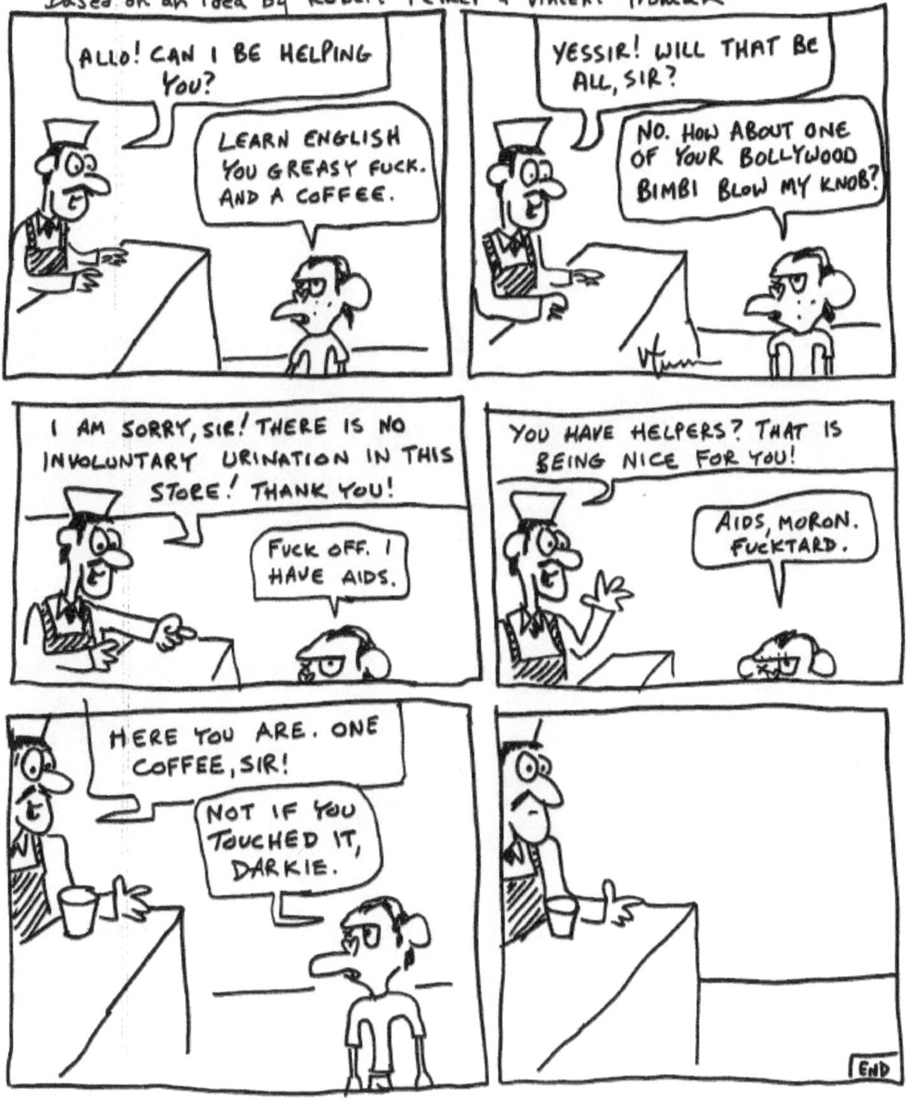

ALLO! CAN I BE HELPING YOU?
LEARN ENGLISH YOU GREASY FUCK. AND A COFFEE.
YESSIR! WILL THAT BE ALL, SIR?
NO. HOW ABOUT ONE OF YOUR BOLLYWOOD BIMBI BLOW MY KNOB?
I AM SORRY, SIR! THERE IS NO INVOLUNTARY URINATION IN THIS STORE! THANK YOU!
FUCK OFF. I HAVE AIDS.
YOU HAVE HELPERS? THAT IS BEING NICE FOR YOU!
AIDS, MORON. FUCKTARD.
HERE YOU ARE. ONE COFFEE, SIR!
NOT IF YOU TOUCHED IT, DARKIE.
END

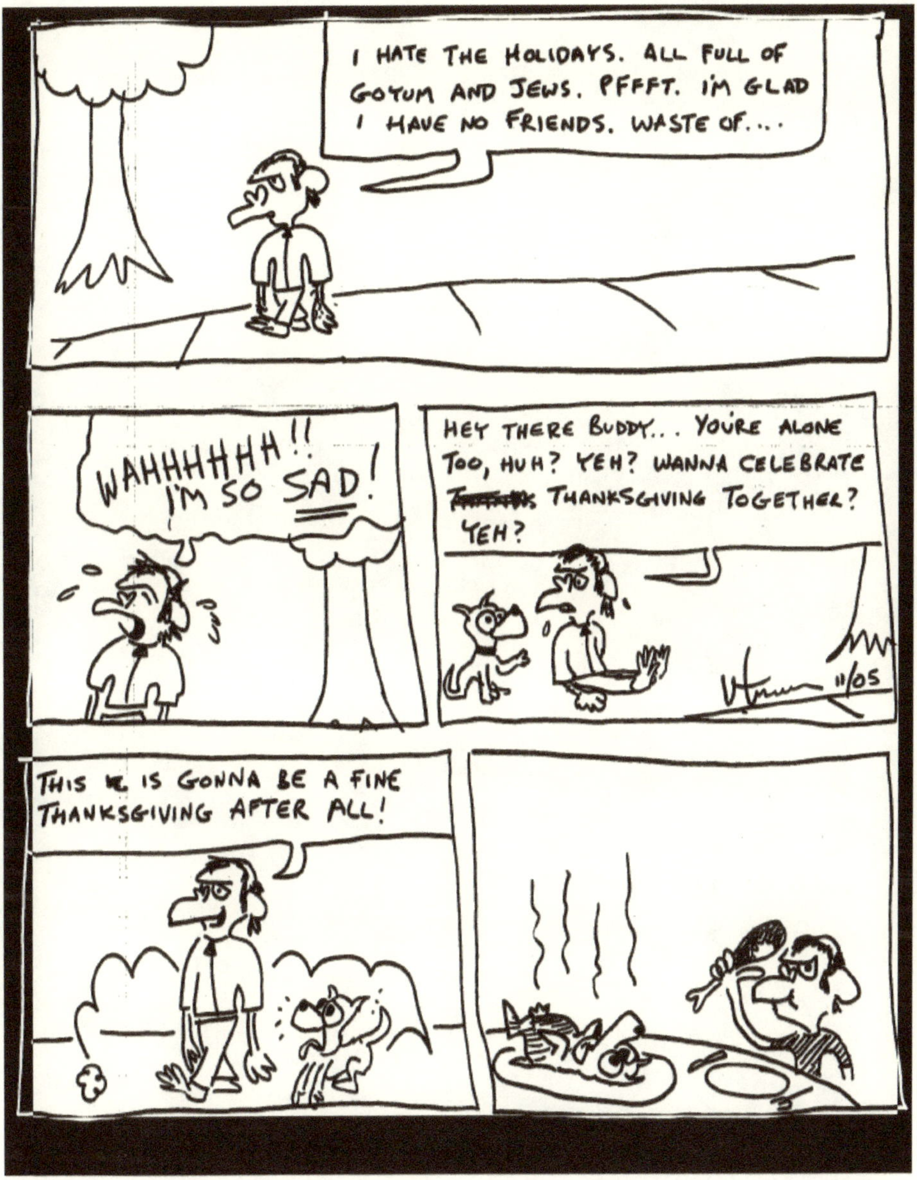
I HATE THE HOLIDAYS. ALL FULL OF GOYUM AND JEWS. PFFFT. I'M GLAD I HAVE NO FRIENDS. WASTE OF...
WAHHHHHH!! I'M SO SAD!
HEY THERE BUDDY... YOU'RE ALONE TOO, HUH? YEH? WANNA CELEBRATE THANKSGIVING TOGETHER? YEH?
11/05
THIS IS GONNA BE A FINE THANKSGIVING AFTER ALL!

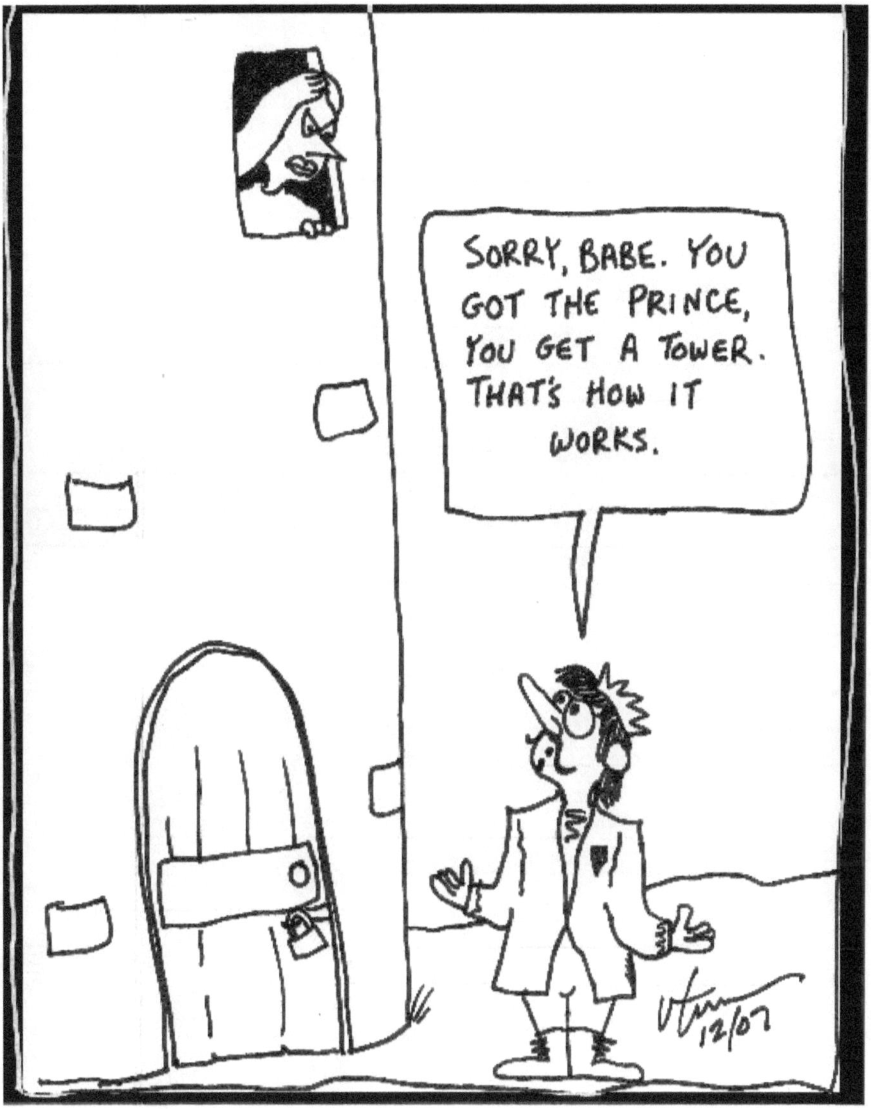
SORRY, BABE. YOU GOT THE PRINCE, YOU GET A TOWER. THAT'S HOW IT WORKS.

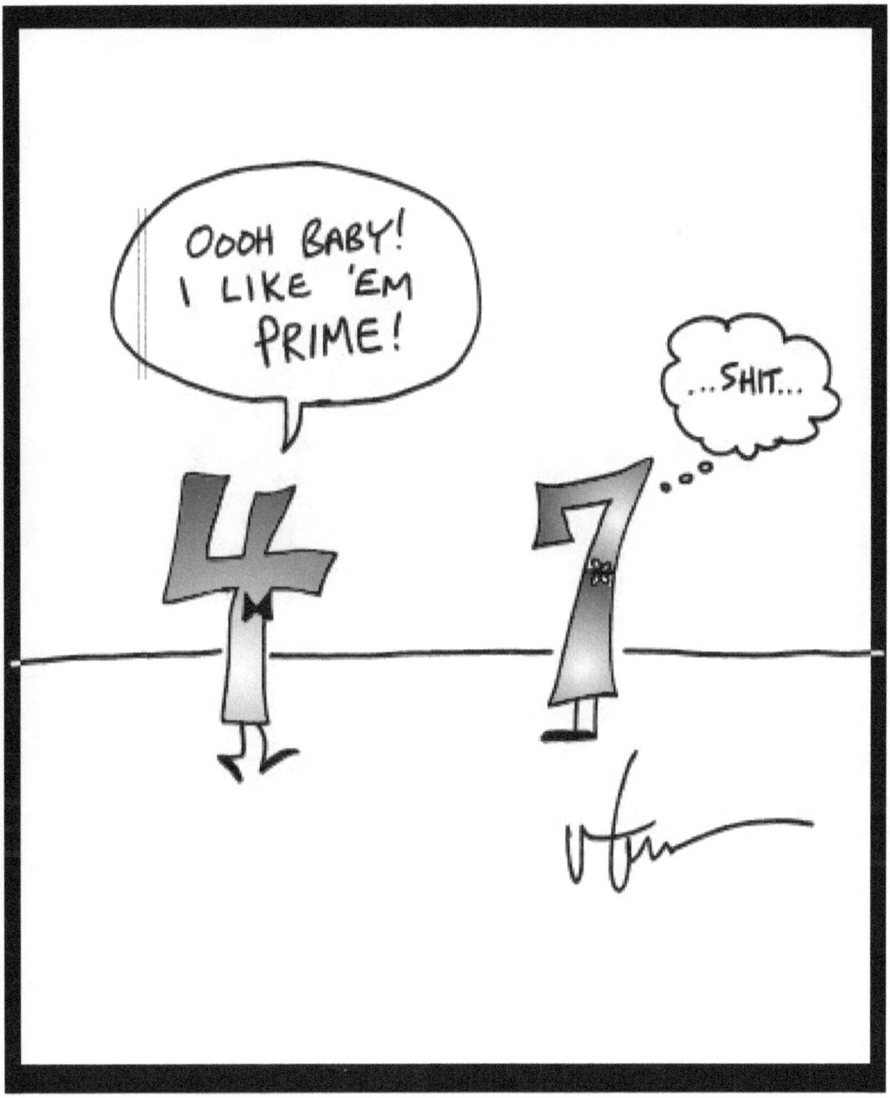
OOOH BABY! I LIKE 'EM PRIME!
...SHIT...

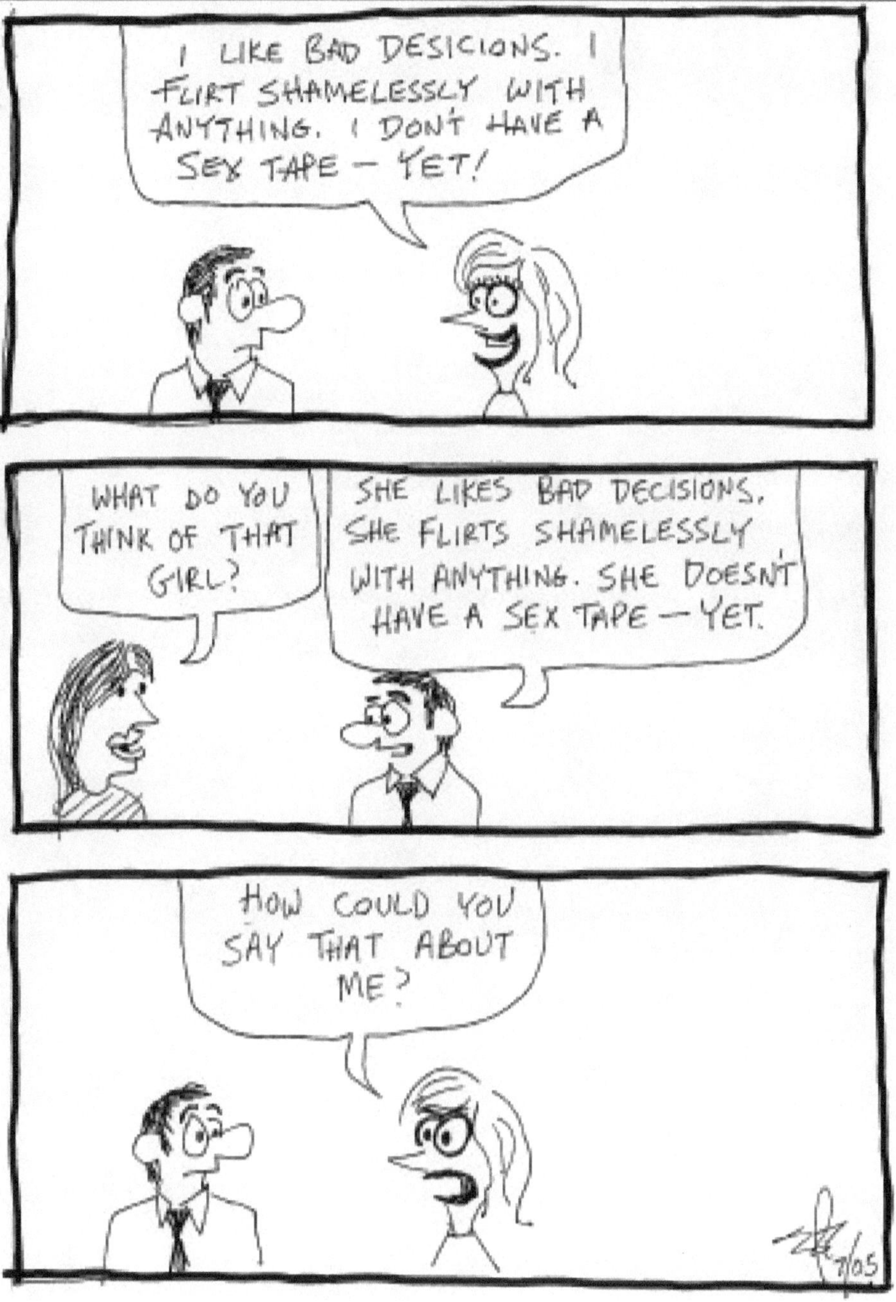
I LIKE BAD DESICIONS. I FLIRT SHAMELESSLY WITH ANYTHING. I DON'T HAVE A SEX TAPE — YET!
WHAT DO YOU THINK OF THAT GIRL?
SHE LIKES BAD DECISIONS. SHE FLIRTS SHAMELESSLY WITH ANYTHING. SHE DOESN'T HAVE A SEX TAPE — YET.
HOW COULD YOU SAY THAT ABOUT ME?
7/05

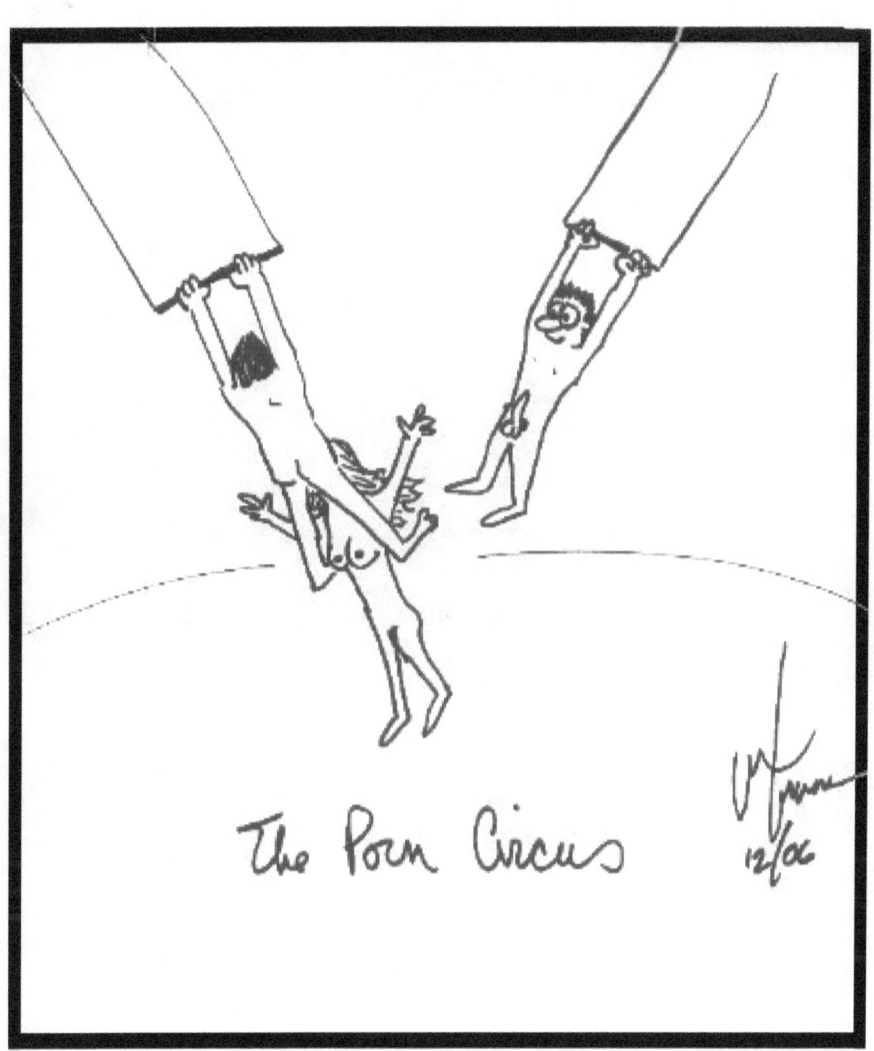

The Porn Circus

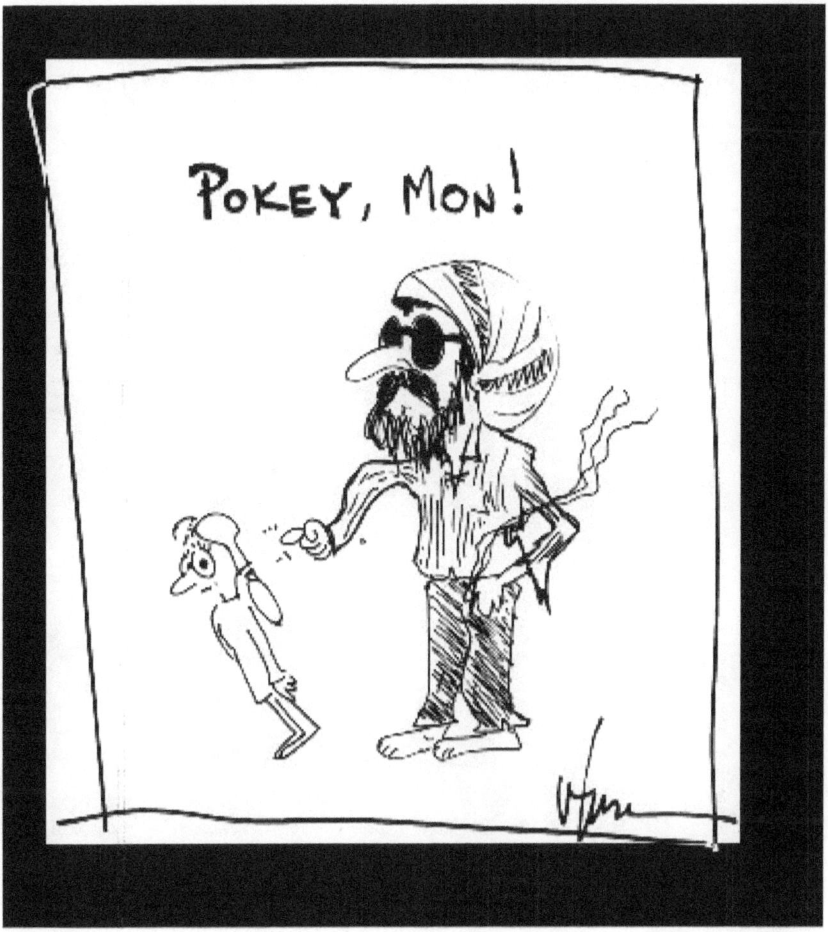
POKEY, MON!

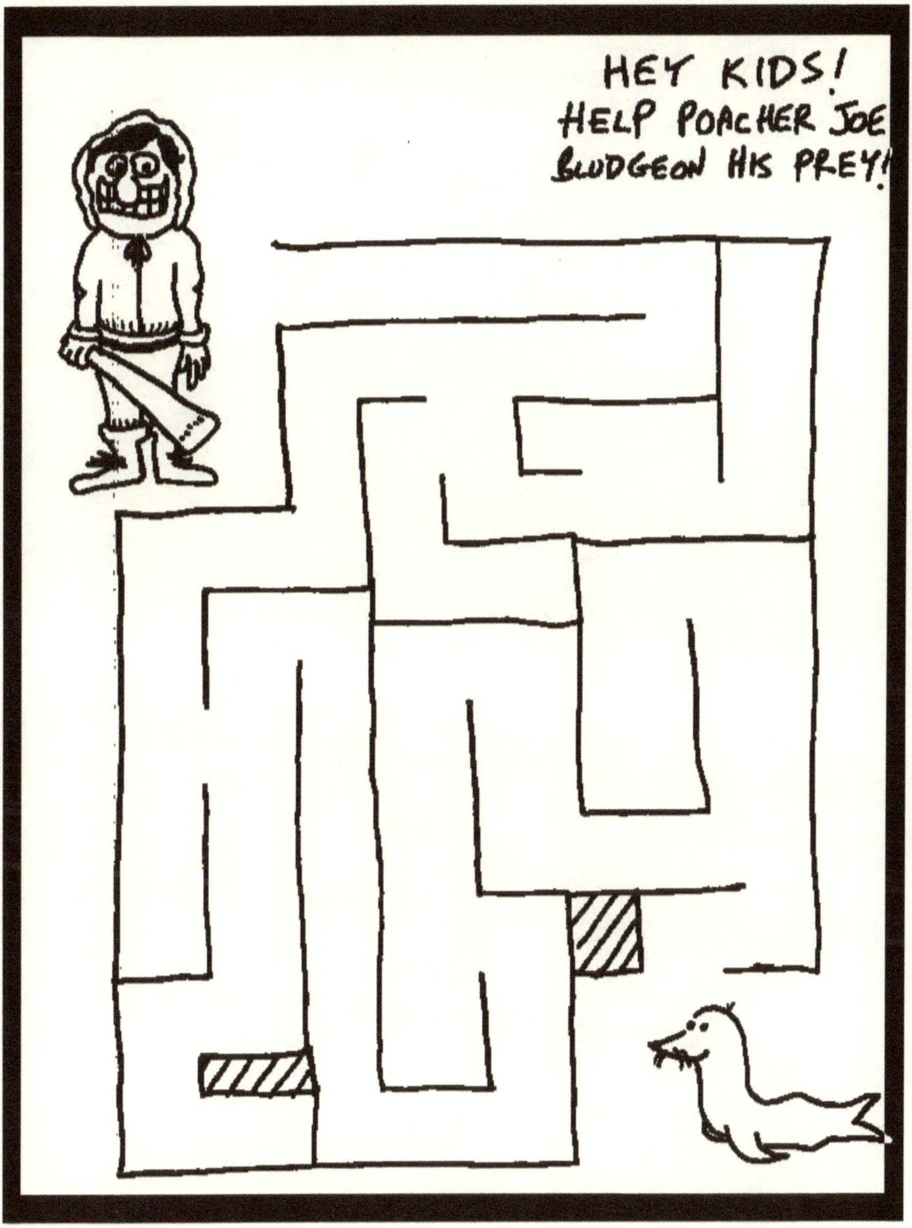
HEY KIDS!
HELP POACHER JOE
BLUDGEON HIS PREY!

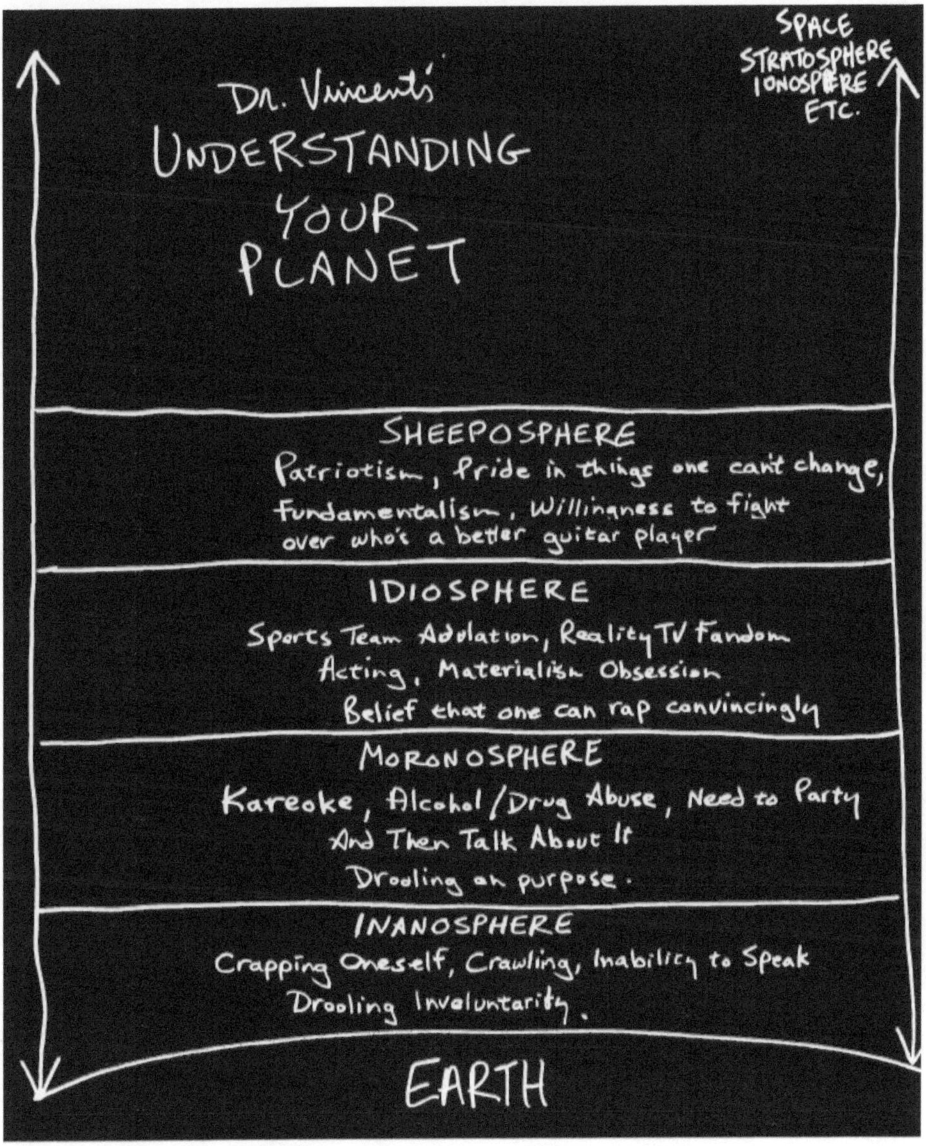
SPACE
STRATOSPHERE
IONOSPHERE
ETC.
Dr. Vincent's
UNDERSTANDING YOUR PLANET
SHEEPOSPHERE
Patriotism, Pride in things one can't change, Fundamentalism, Willingness to fight over who's a better guitar player
IDIOSPHERE
Sports Team Adulation, Reality TV Fandom Acting, Materialism Obsession Belief that one can rap convincingly
MORONOSPHERE
Kareoke, Alcohol/Drug Abuse, Need to Party And Then Talk About It Drooling on purpose.
INANOSPHERE
Crapping Oneself, Crawling, Inability to Speak Drooling Involuntarily.
EARTH

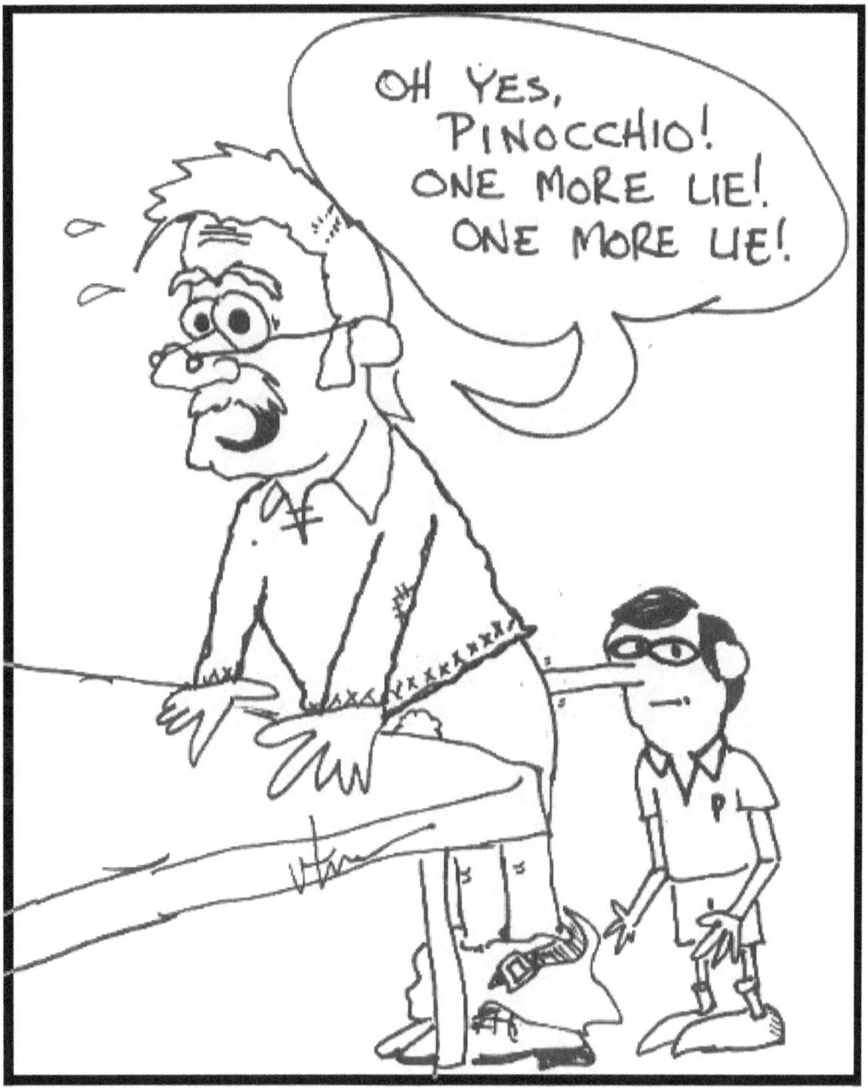
OH YES, PINOCCHIO! ONE MORE LIE! ONE MORE LIE!

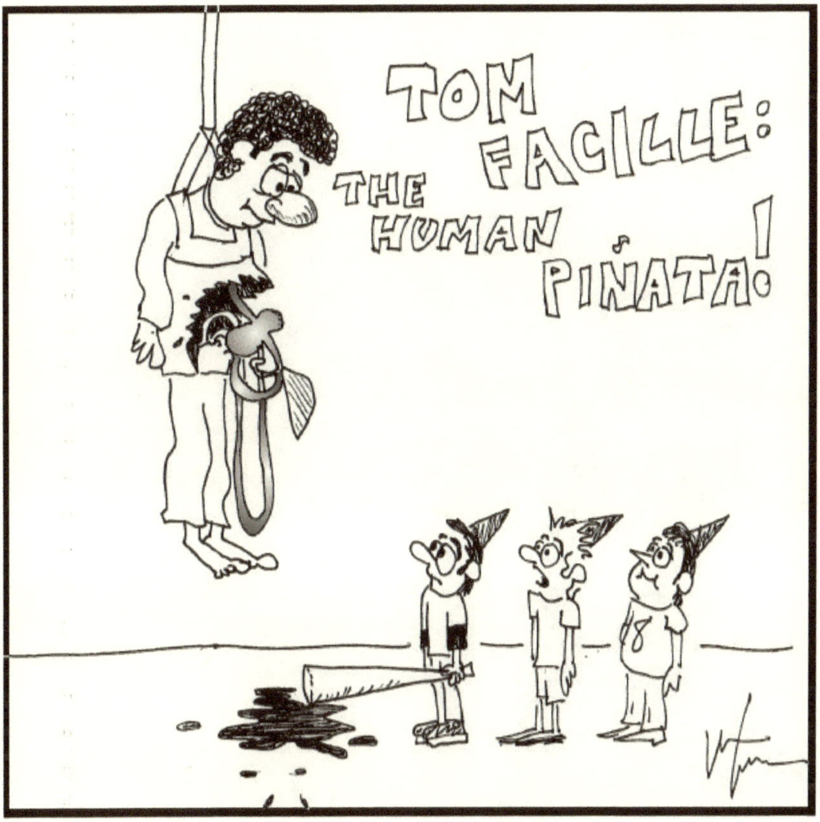
TOM FACILLE:
THE HUMAN PIÑATA!

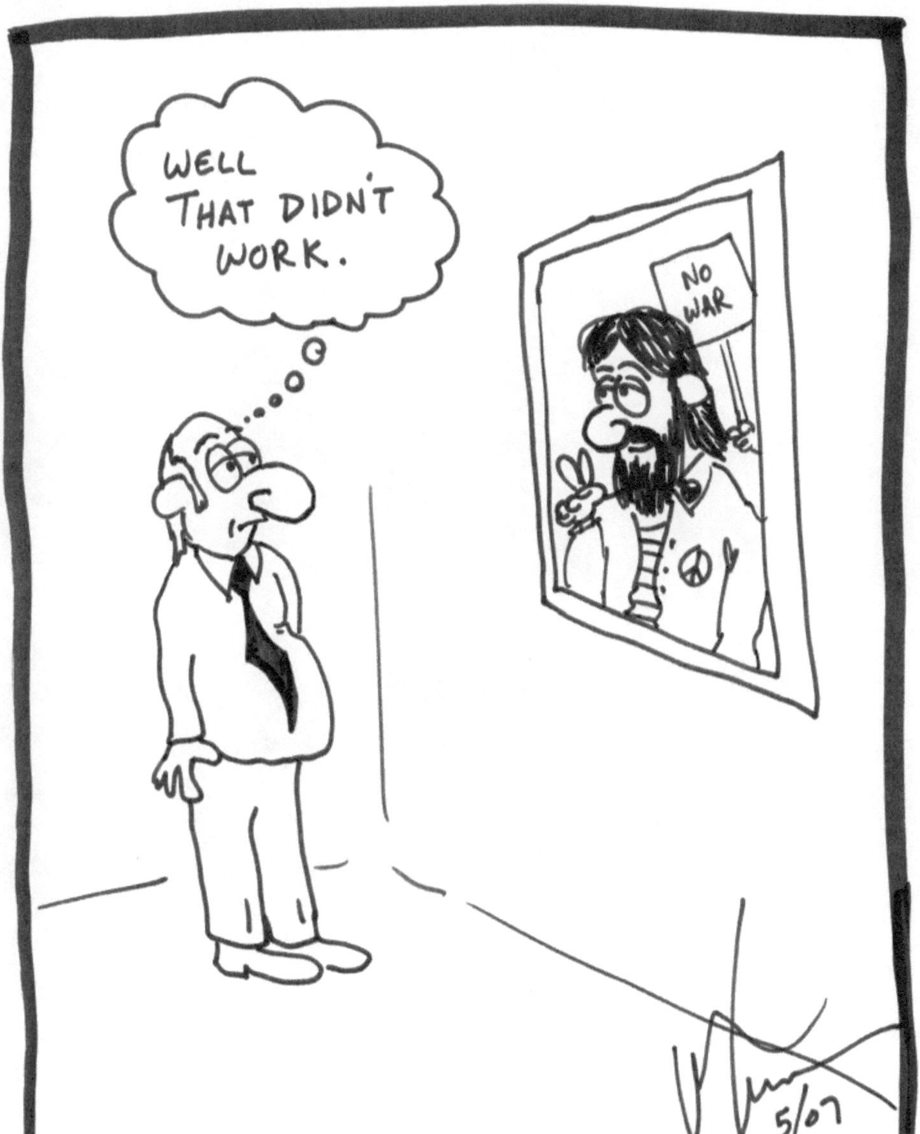
WELL THAT DIDN'T WORK.
NO WAR
5/07

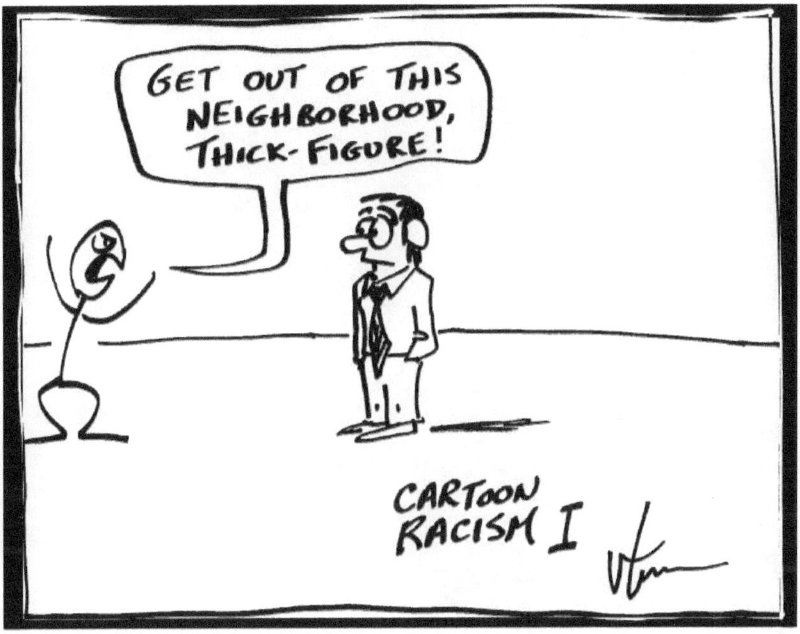
GET OUT OF THIS NEIGHBORHOOD, THICK-FIGURE!
CARTOON RACISM I

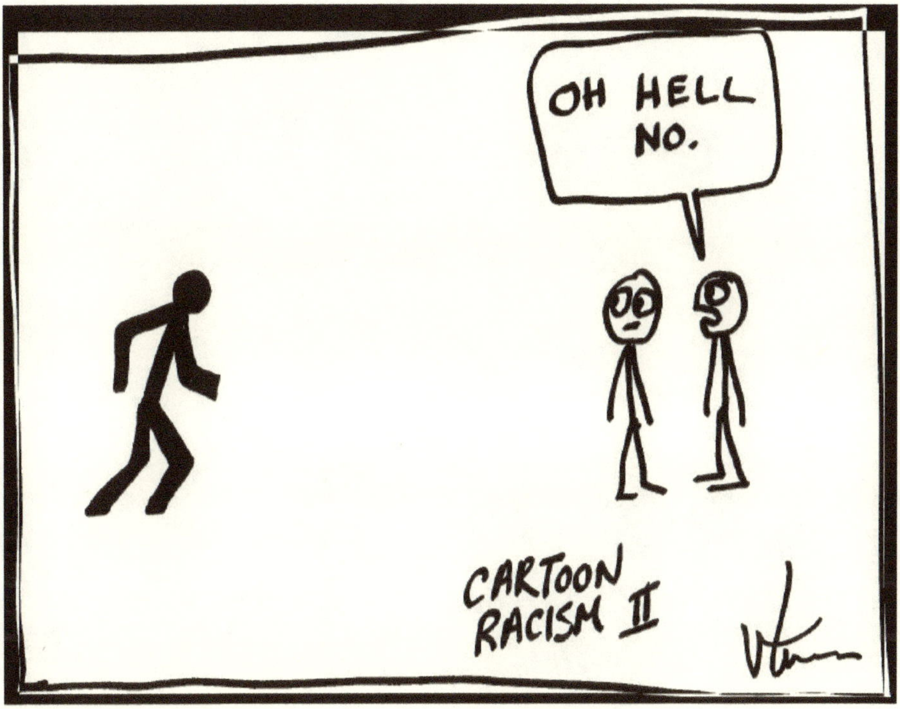
OH HELL NO.
CARTOON RACISM II

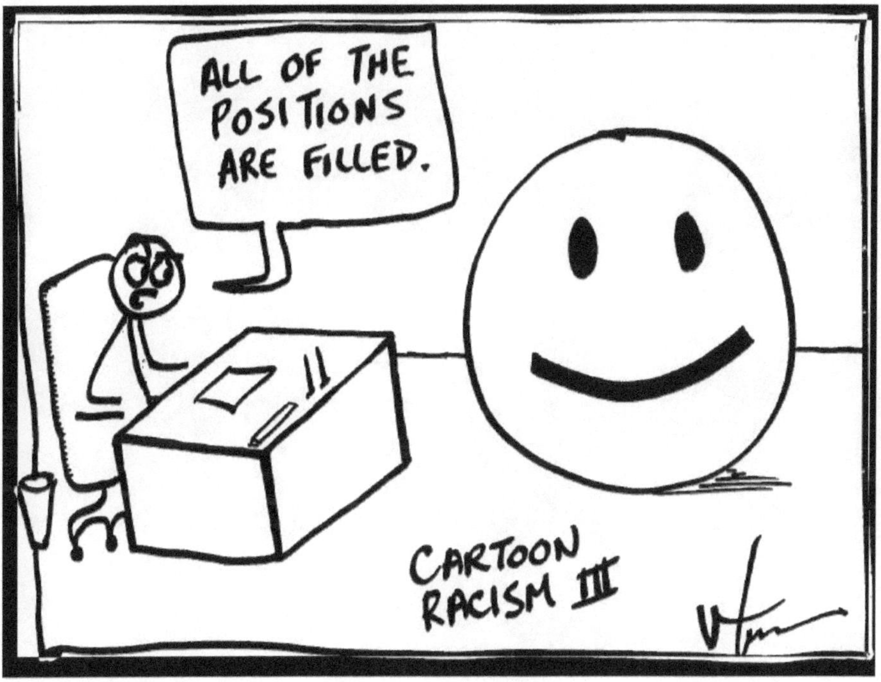
ALL OF THE POSITIONS ARE FILLED.
CARTOON RACISM III

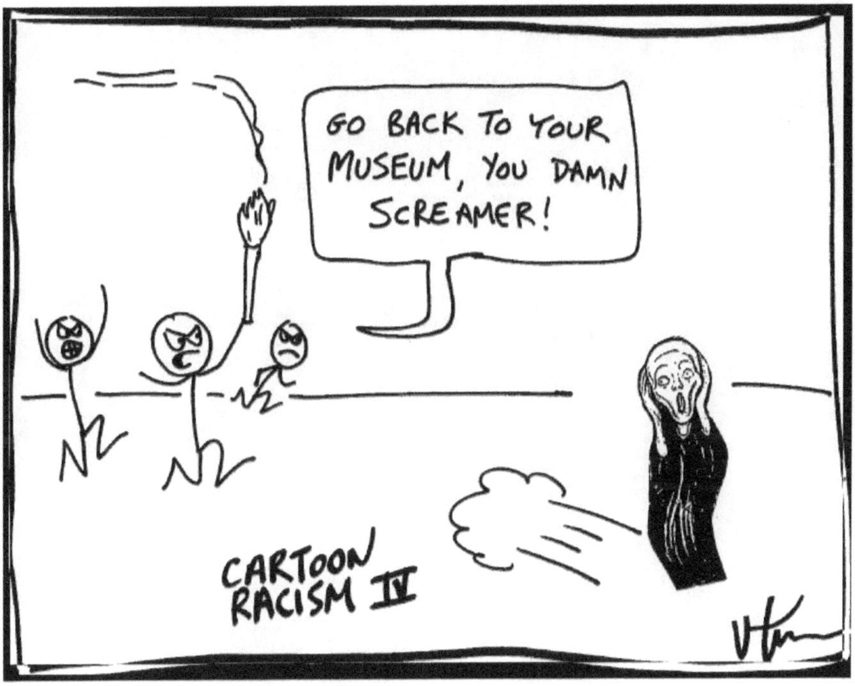
GO BACK TO YOUR MUSEUM, YOU DAMN SCREAMER!
CARTOON RACISM IV

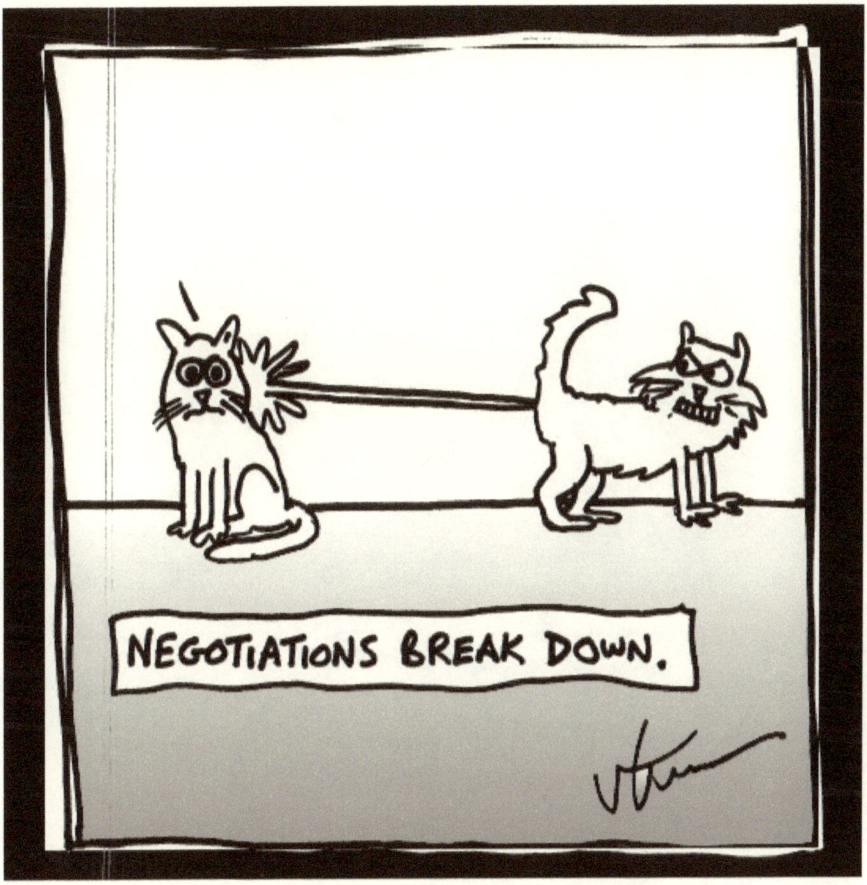
NEGOTIATIONS BREAK DOWN.

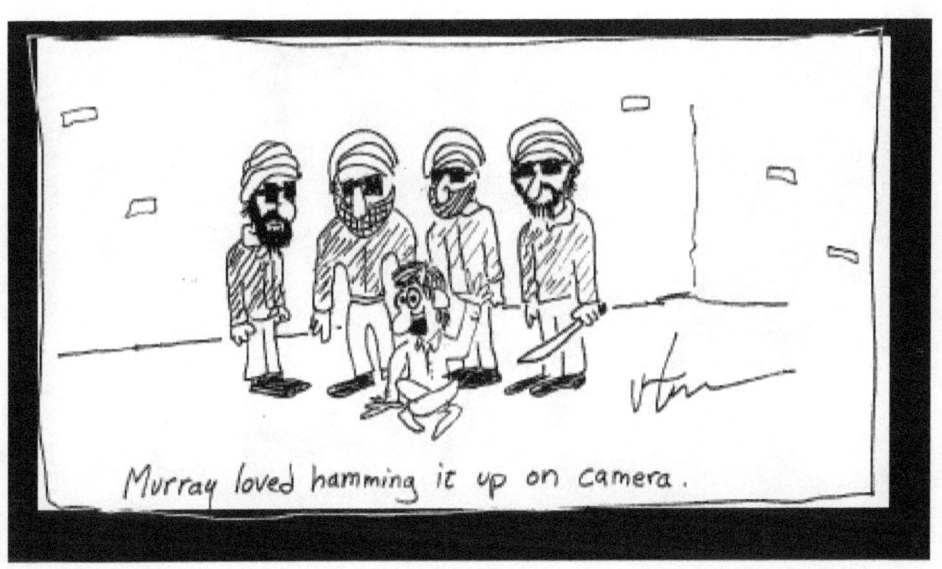

Murray loved hamming it up on camera.

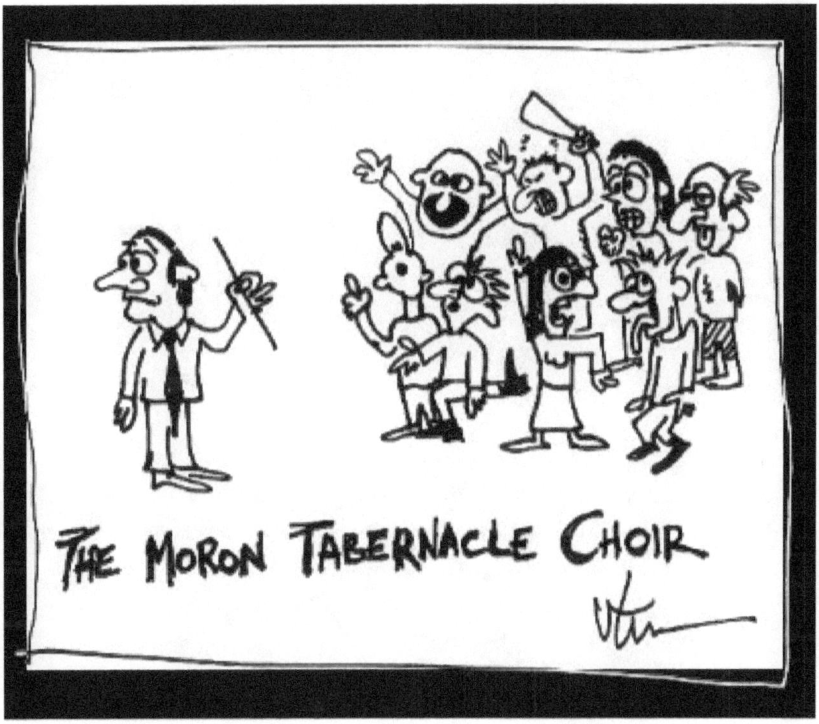
THE MORON TABERNACLE CHOIR

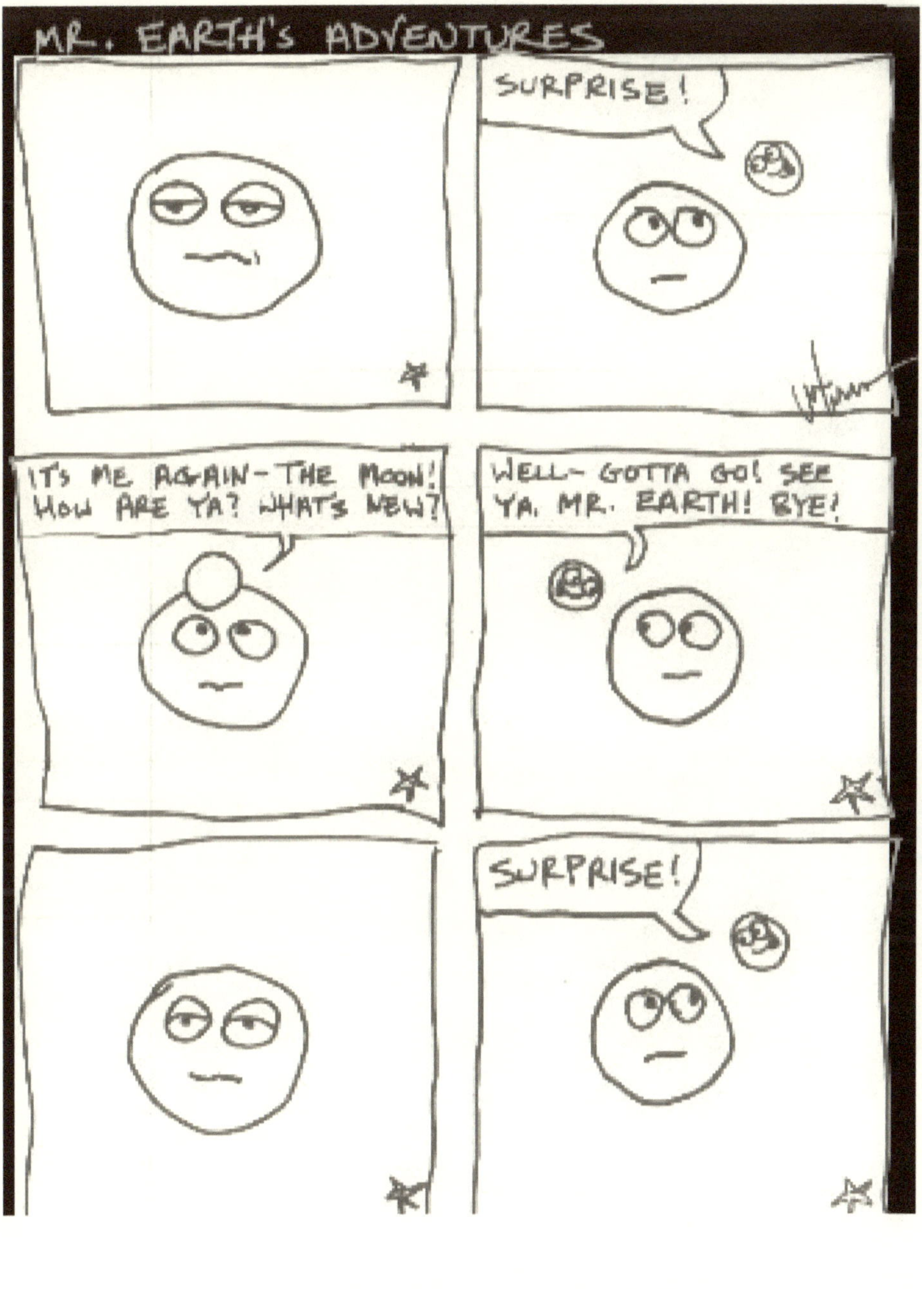
MR. EARTH'S ADVENTURES
SURPRISE!
IT'S ME AGAIN - THE MOON! HOW ARE YA? WHAT'S NEW?
WELL- GOTTA GO! SEE YA, MR. EARTH! BYE!
SURPRISE!

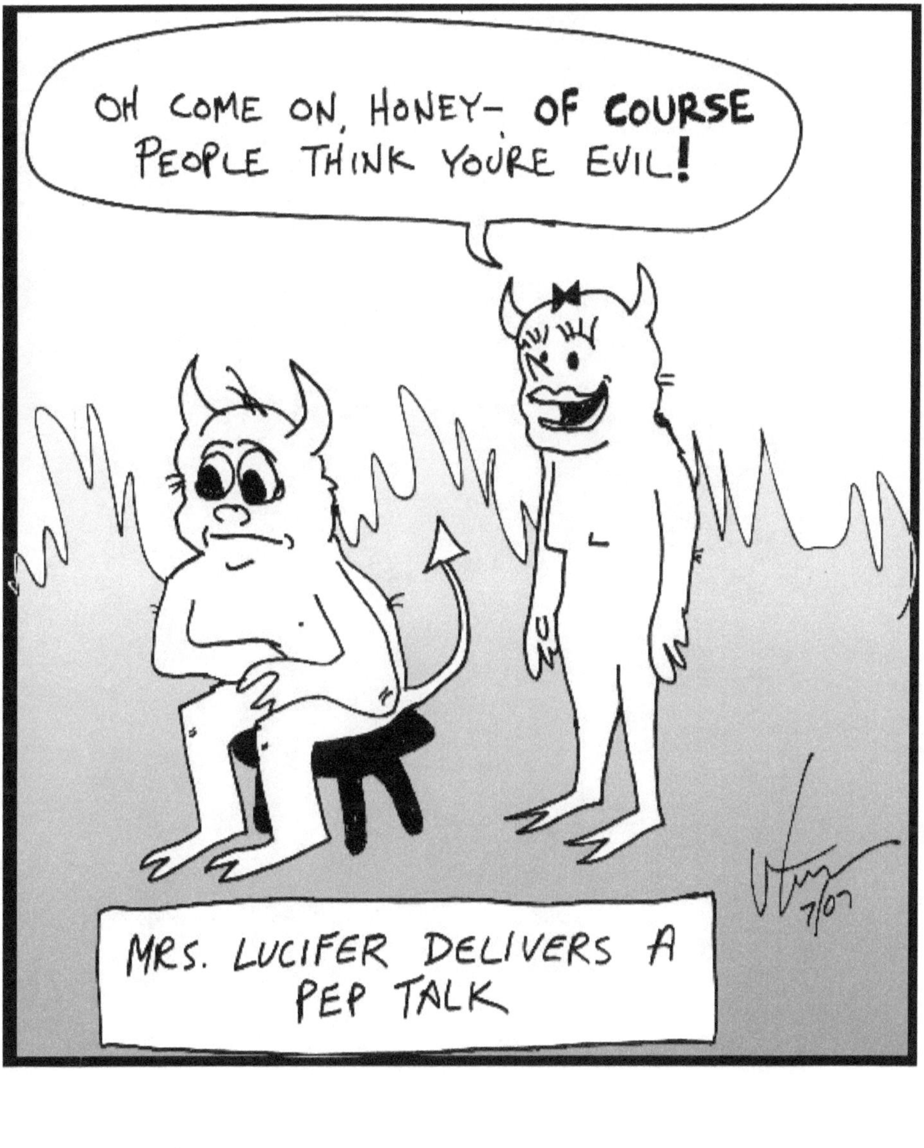
OH COME ON, HONEY- OF COURSE PEOPLE THINK YOU'RE EVIL!
7/07
MRS. LUCIFER DELIVERS A PEP TALK

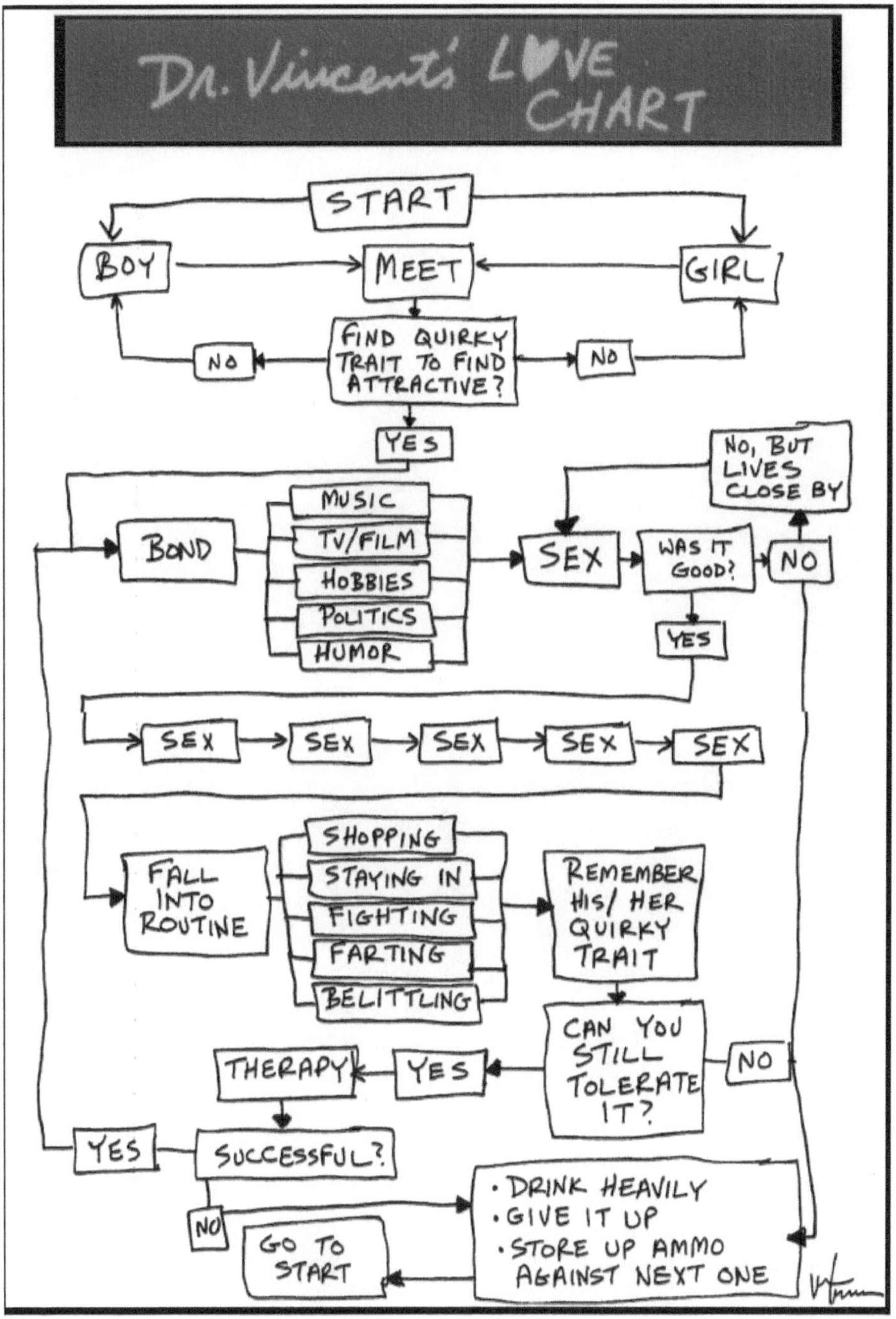
Dr. Vincent's LOVE CHART
START
BOY
MEET
GIRL
FIND QUIRKY TRAIT TO FIND ATTRACTIVE?
NO
NO
YES
NO, BUT LIVES CLOSE BY
BOND
MUSIC
TV/FILM
HOBBIES
POLITICS
HUMOR
SEX
WAS IT GOOD?
NO
YES
SEX
SEX
SEX
SEX
SEX
FALL INTO ROUTINE
SHOPPING
STAYING IN
FIGHTING
FARTING
BELITTLING
REMEMBER HIS/ HER QUIRKY TRAIT
CAN YOU STILL TOLERATE IT?
NO
YES
THERAPY
SUCCESSFUL?
YES
NO
• DRINK HEAVILY
• GIVE IT UP
• STORE UP AMMO AGAINST NEXT ONE
GO TO START

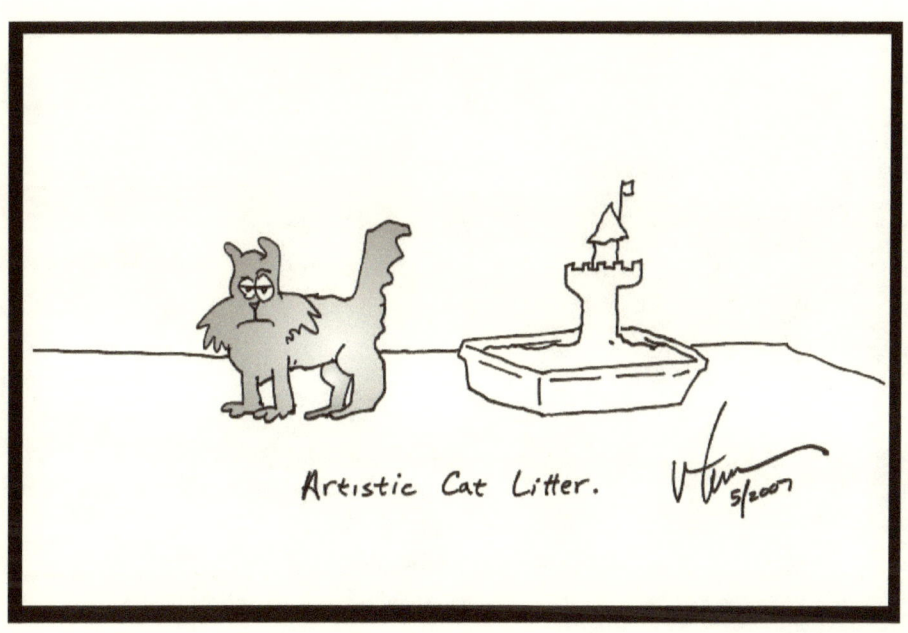

Artistic Cat Litter.

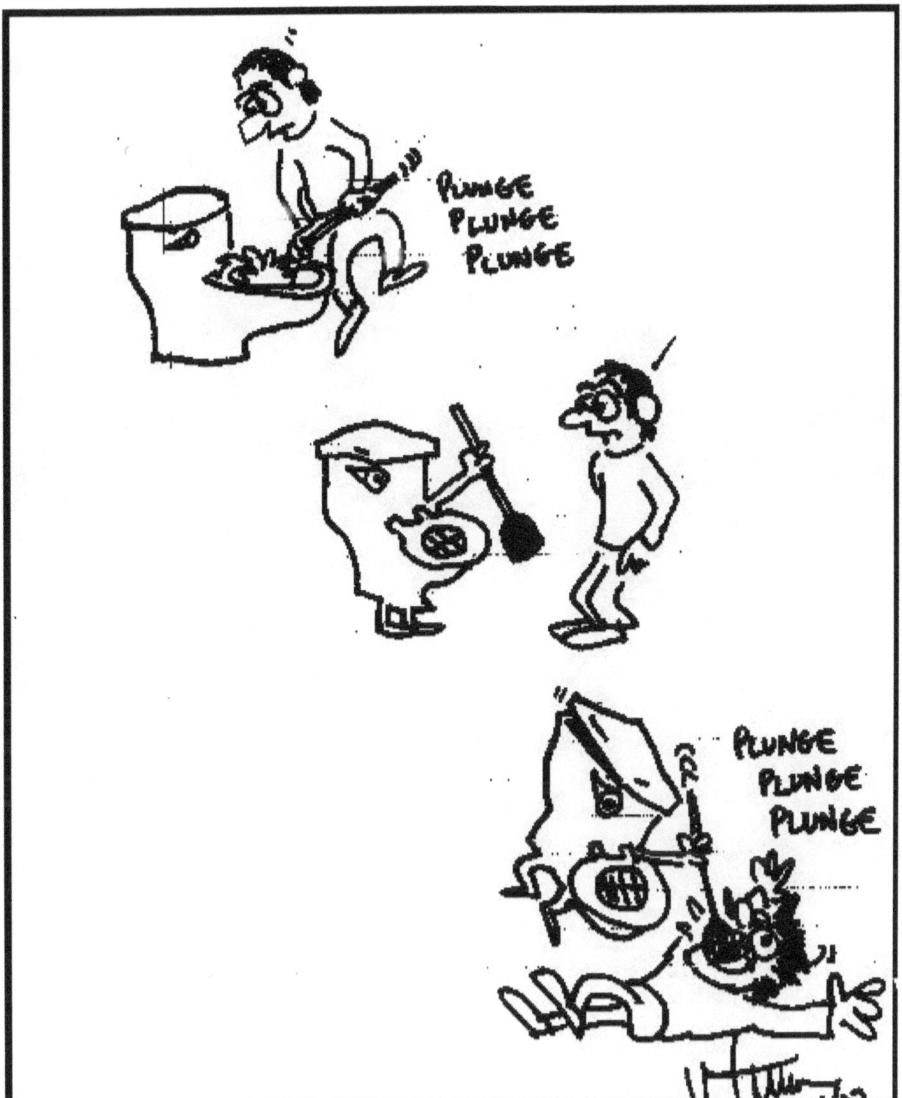
PLUNGE
PLUNGE
PLUNGE
PLUNGE
PLUNGE
PLUNGE

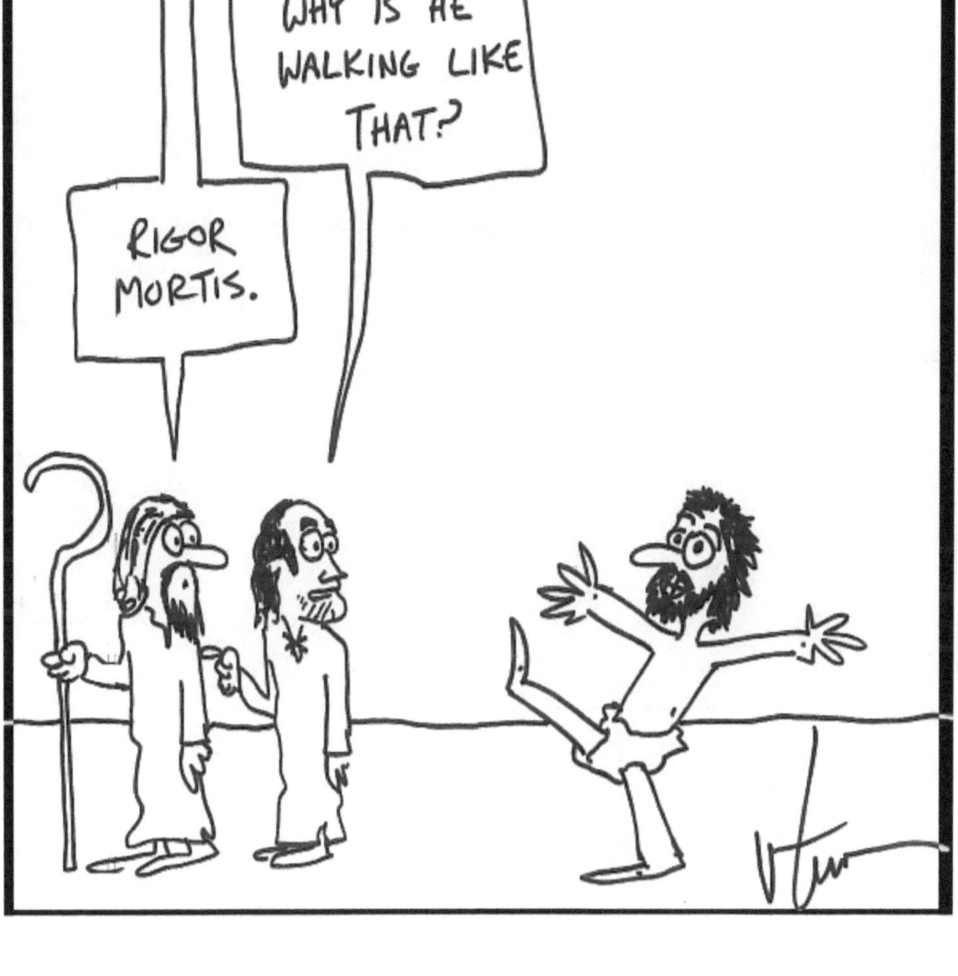
JESUS HAS RISEN!
WHY IS HE WALKING LIKE THAT?
RIGOR MORTIS.

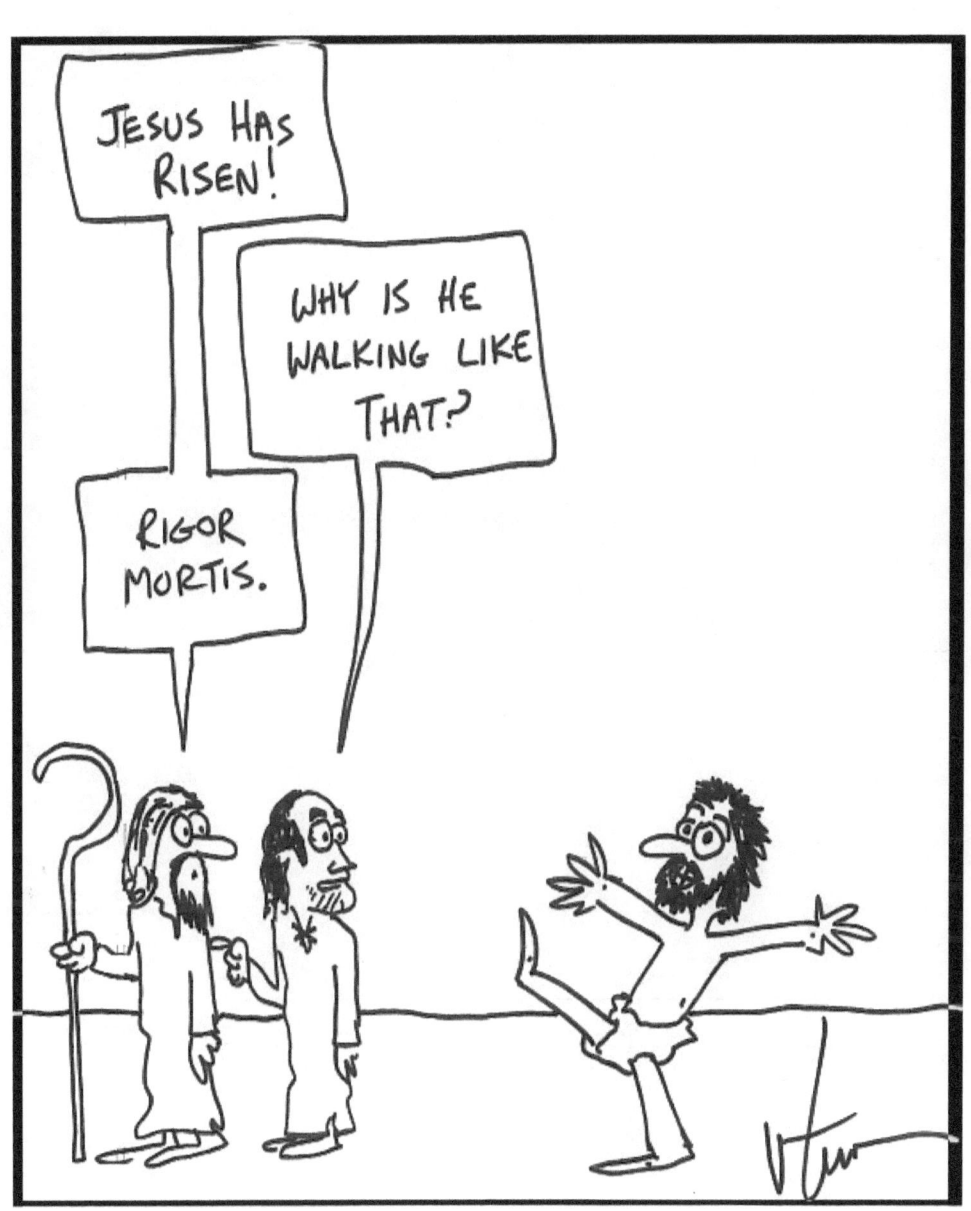

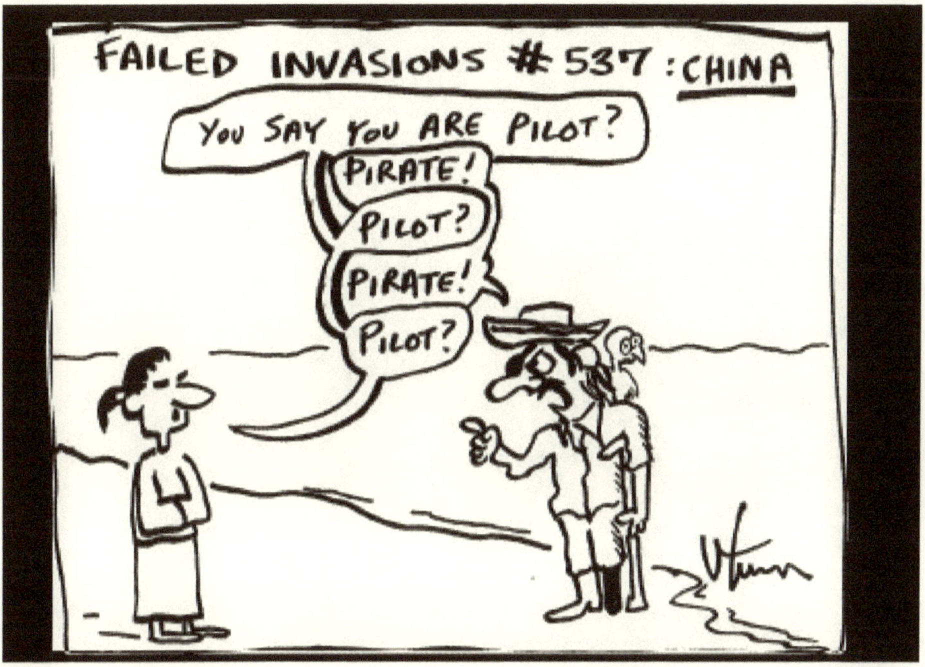
FAILED INVASIONS #537: CHINA
YOU SAY YOU ARE PILOT?
PIRATE!
PILOT?
PIRATE!
PILOT?

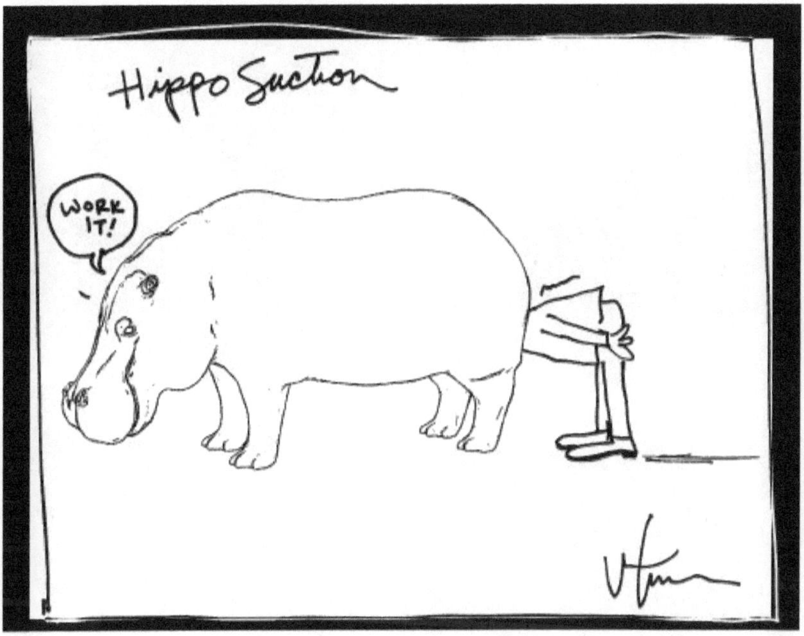
Hippo Suction
WORK IT!

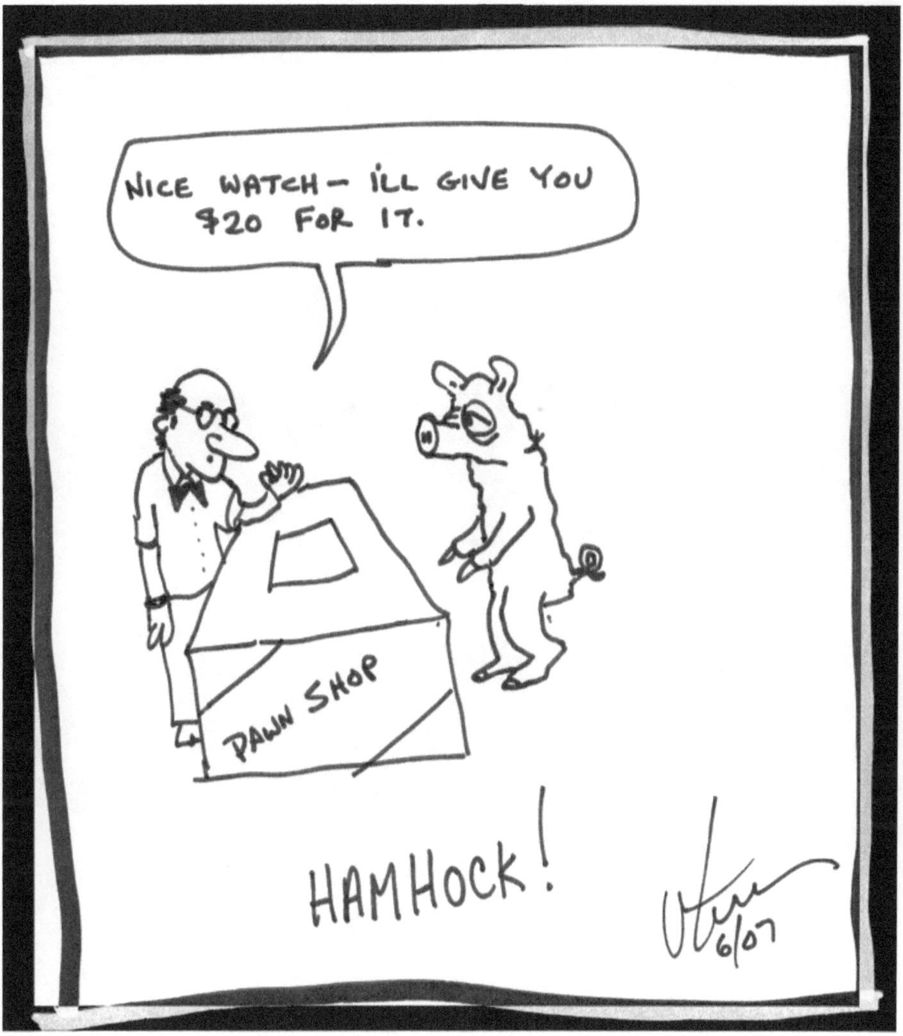
NICE WATCH – I'LL GIVE YOU $20 FOR IT.
PAWN SHOP
HAMHOCK!
6/07

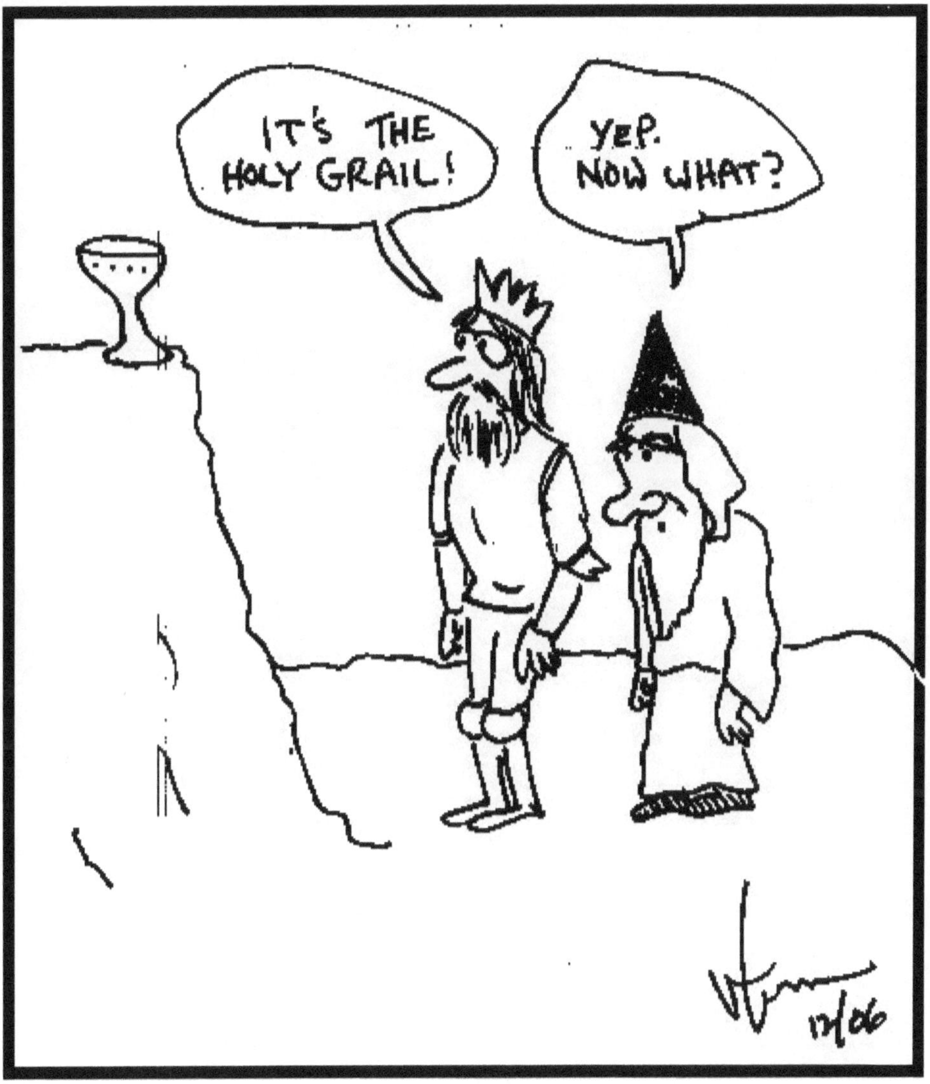
IT'S THE HOLY GRAIL!
YEP. NOW WHAT?

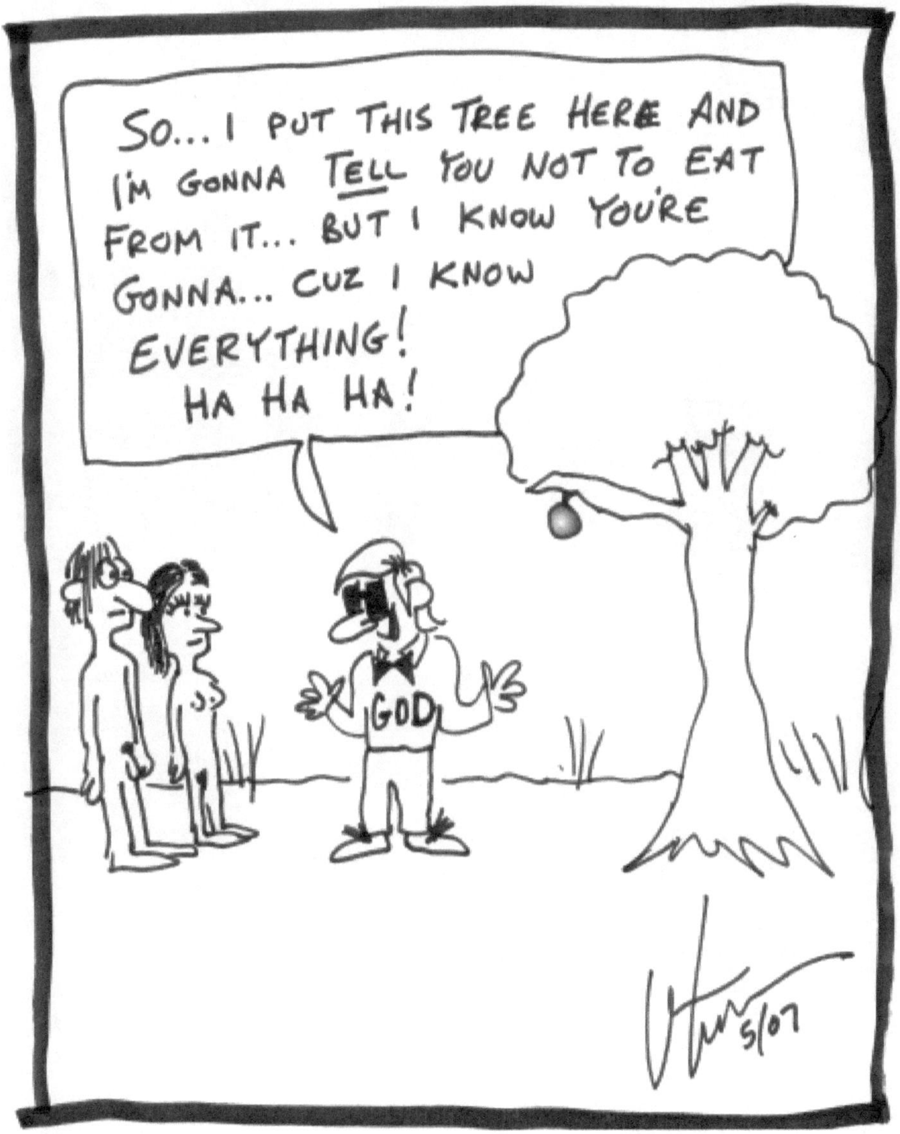
SO... I PUT THIS TREE HERE AND I'M GONNA TELL YOU NOT TO EAT FROM IT... BUT I KNOW YOU'RE GONNA... CUZ I KNOW EVERYTHING! HA HA HA!
GOD
5/07

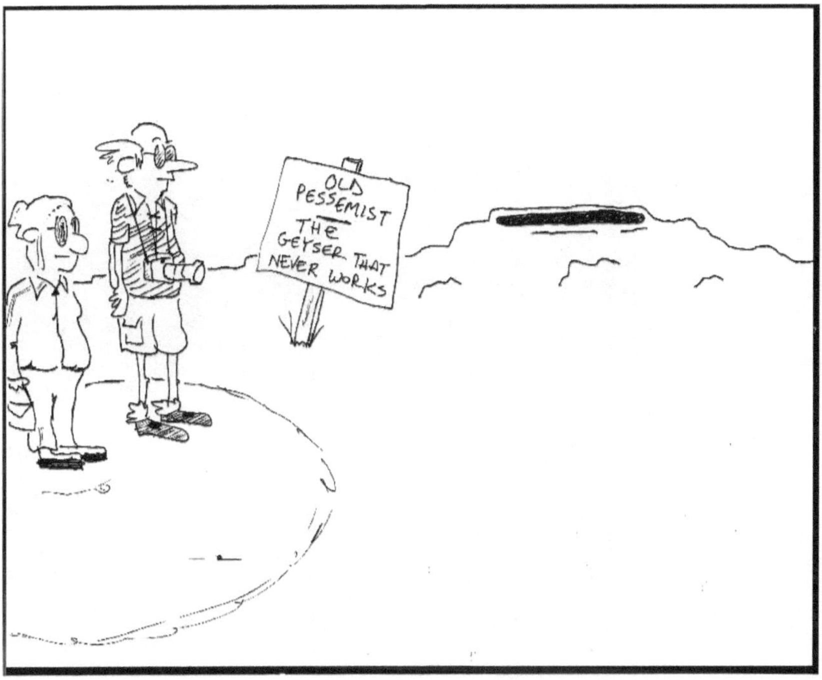
OLD PESSEMIST
THE GEYSER THAT NEVER WORKS

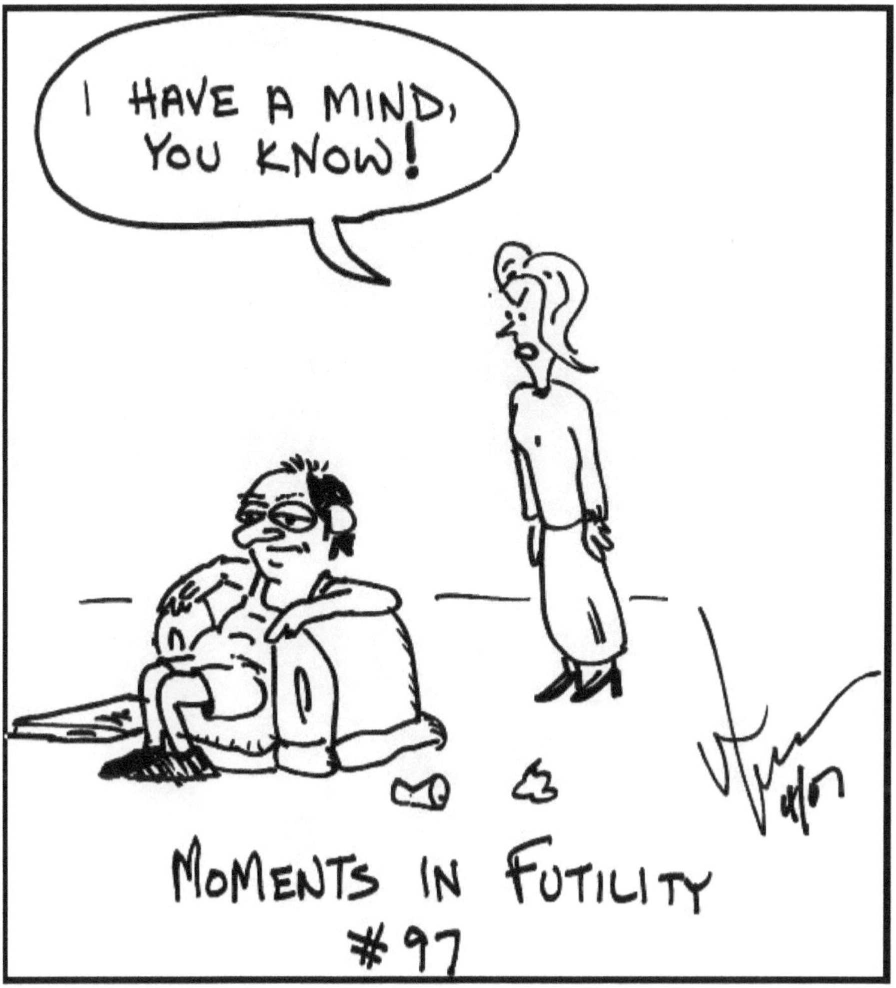
I HAVE A MIND, YOU KNOW!
MOMENTS IN FUTILITY #97

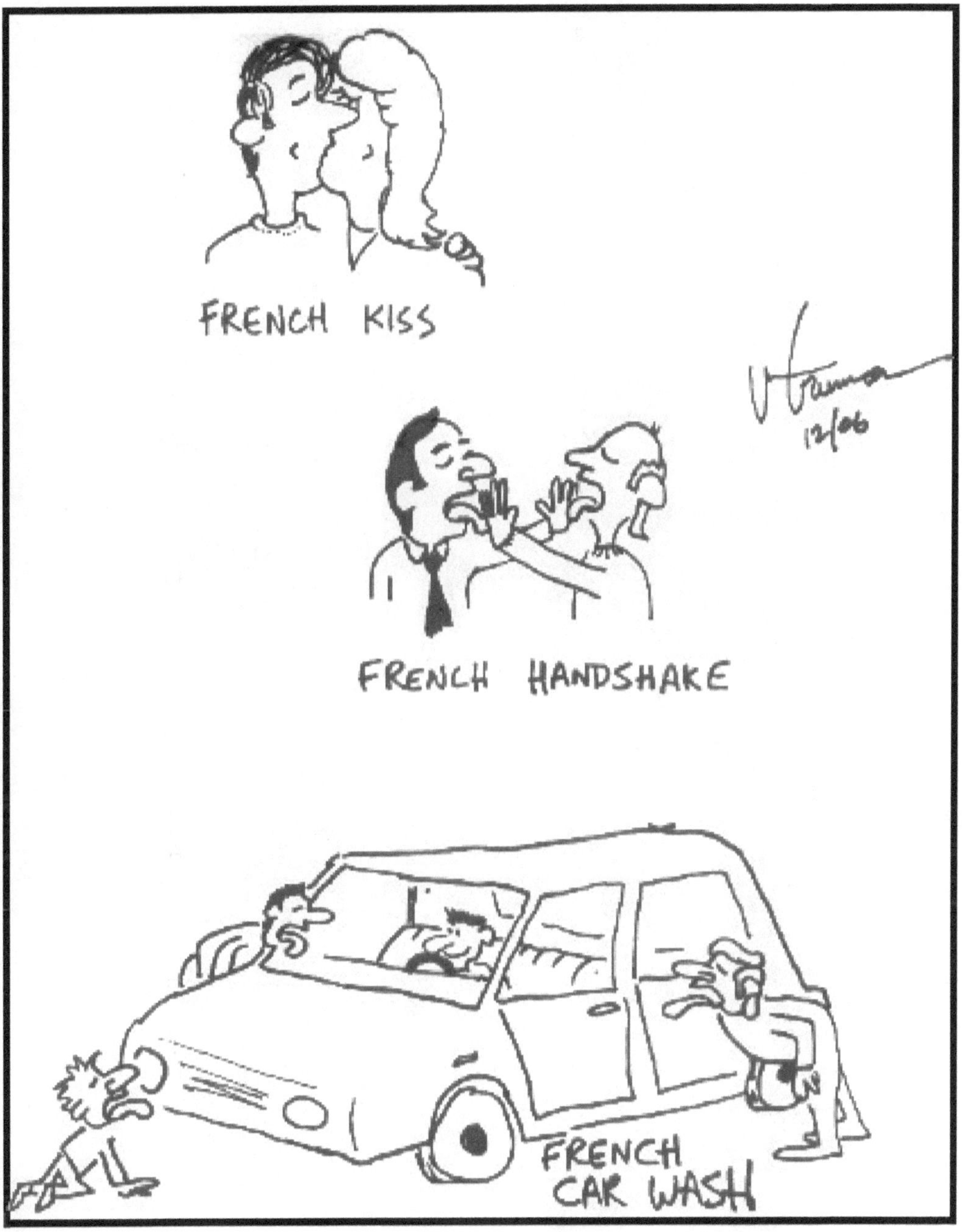
FRENCH KISS
FRENCH HANDSHAKE
FRENCH
CAR WASH
12/06

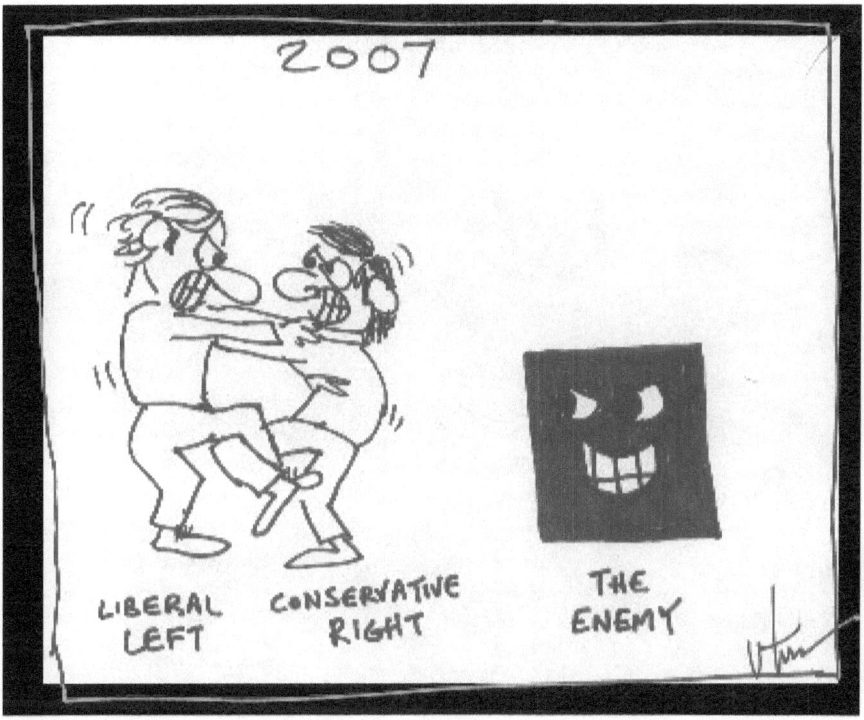
2007
LIBERAL
LEFT
CONSERVATIVE
RIGHT
THE
ENEMY

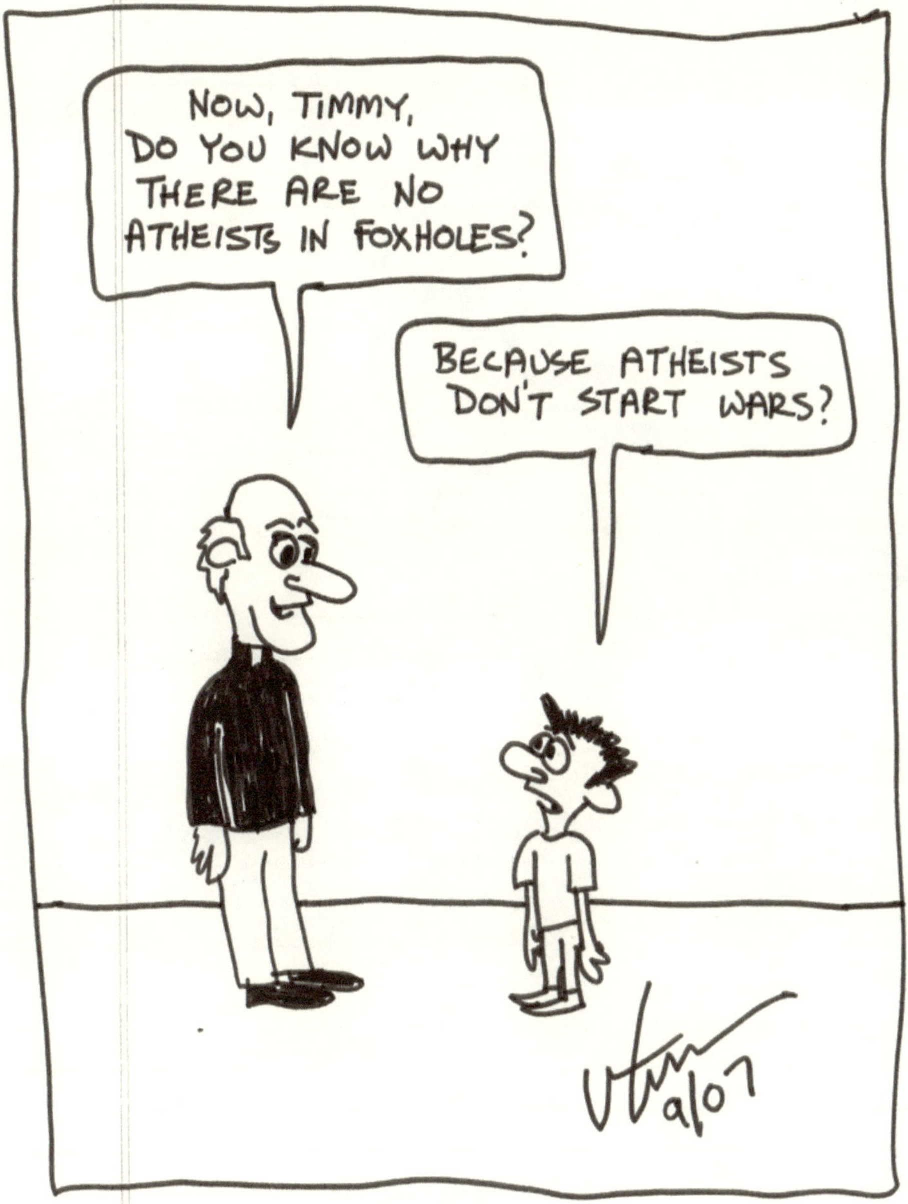
NOW, TIMMY,
DO YOU KNOW WHY
THERE ARE NO
ATHEISTS IN FOXHOLES?
BECAUSE ATHEISTS
DON'T START WARS?
9/07

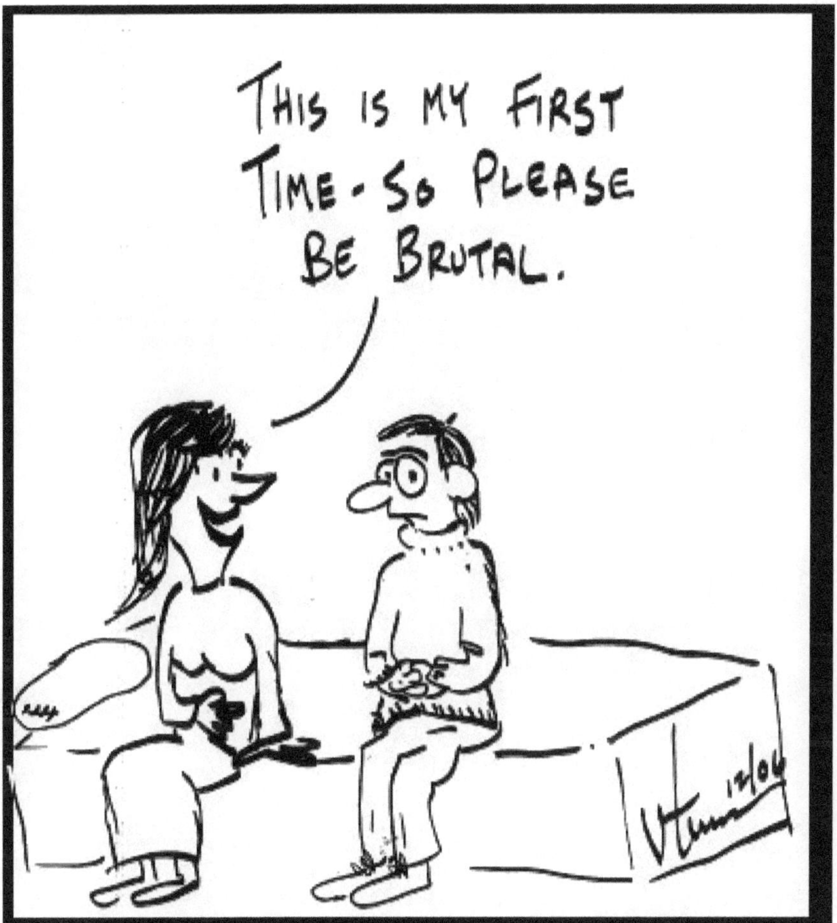
THIS IS MY FIRST TIME - SO PLEASE BE BRUTAL.

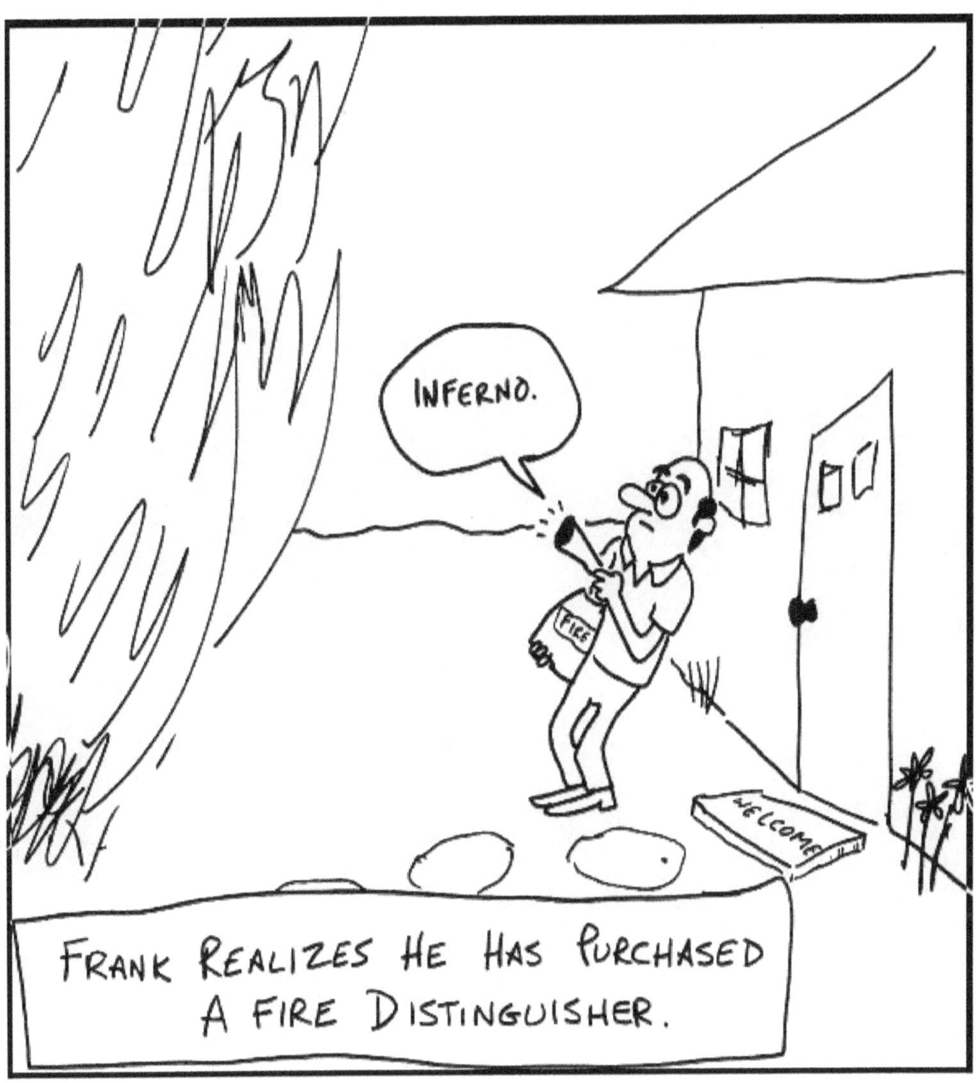
INFERNO.
FIRE
WELCOME
FRANK REALIZES HE HAS PURCHASED A FIRE DISTINGUISHER.

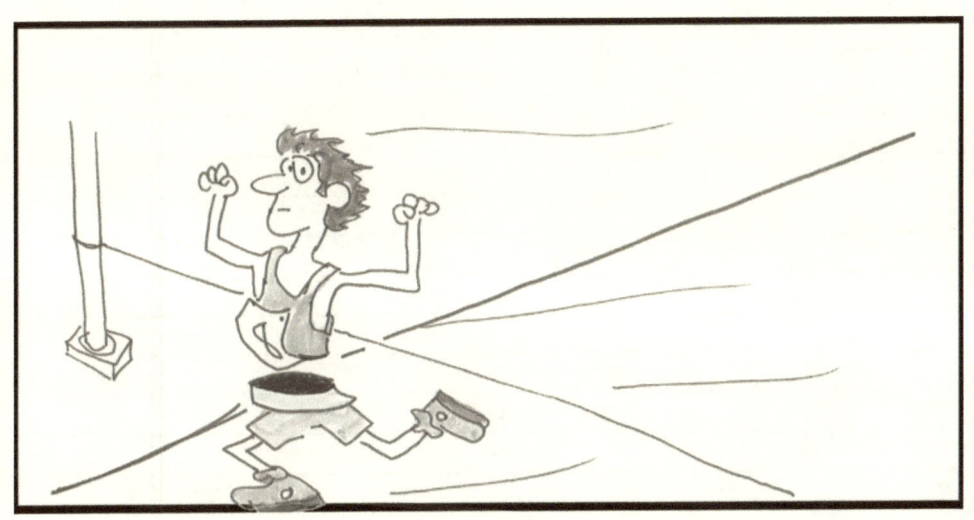

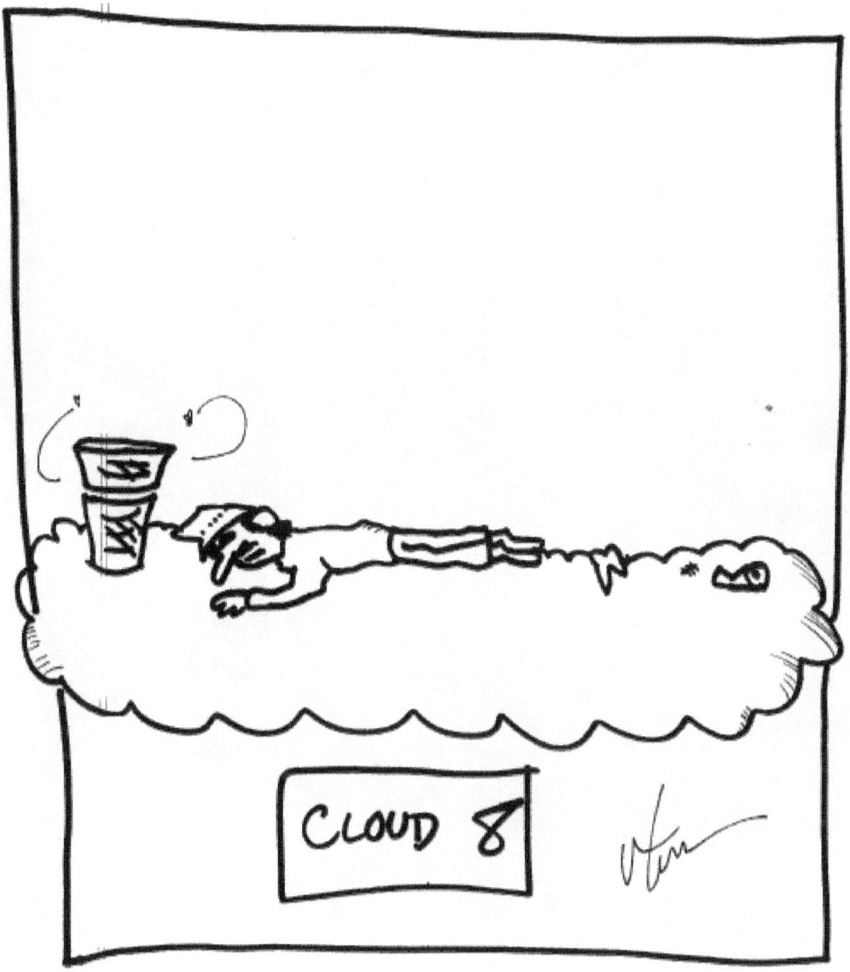
CLOUD 8

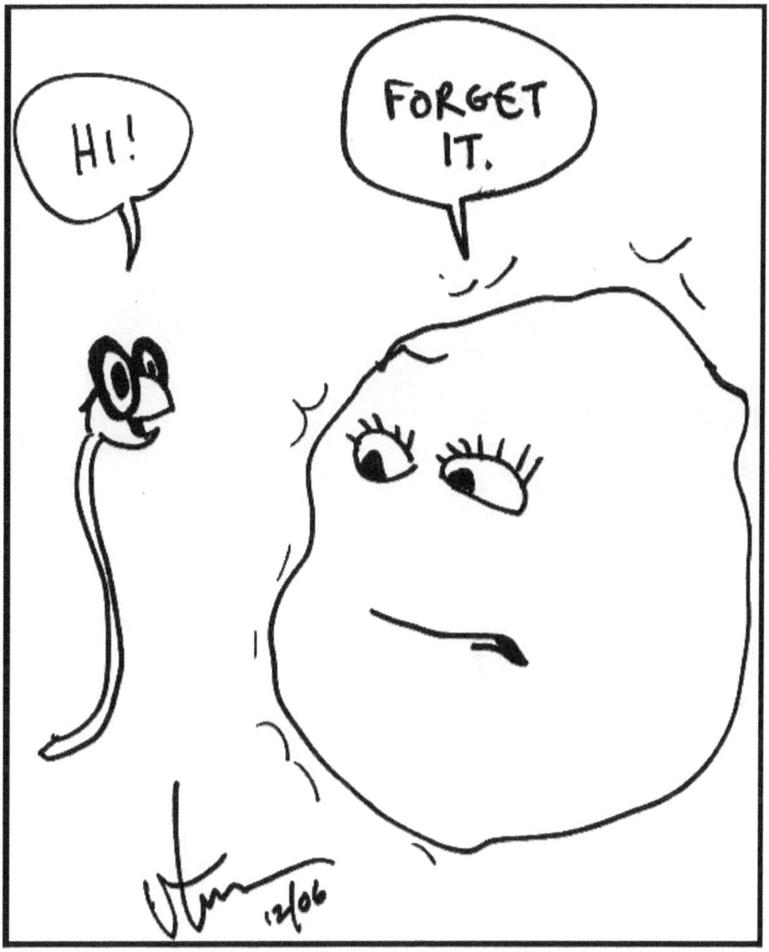
HI!
FORGET IT.
12/06

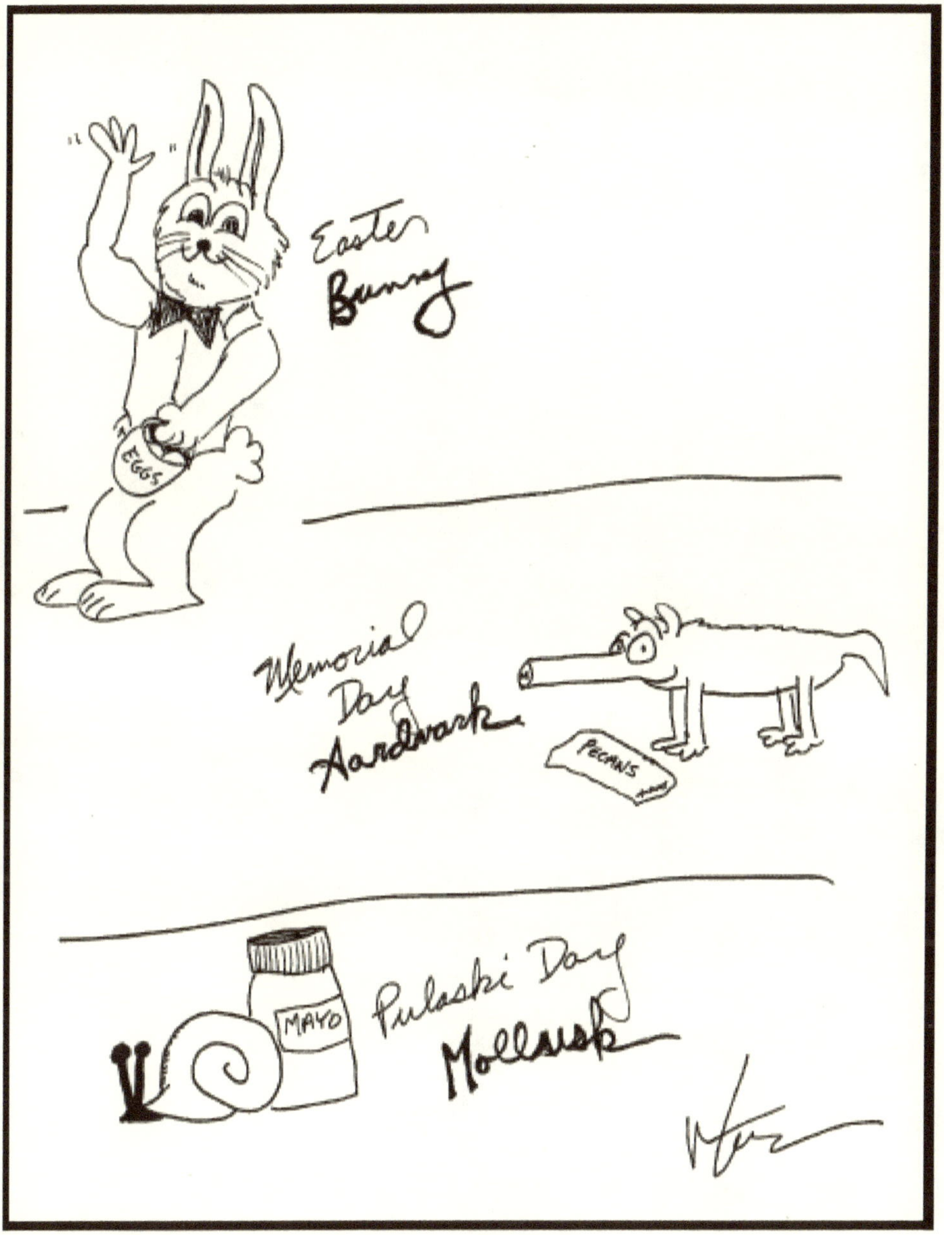
Easter Bunny
EGGS
Memorial Day Aardvark
PECANS
Pulaski Day Mollusk
MAYO

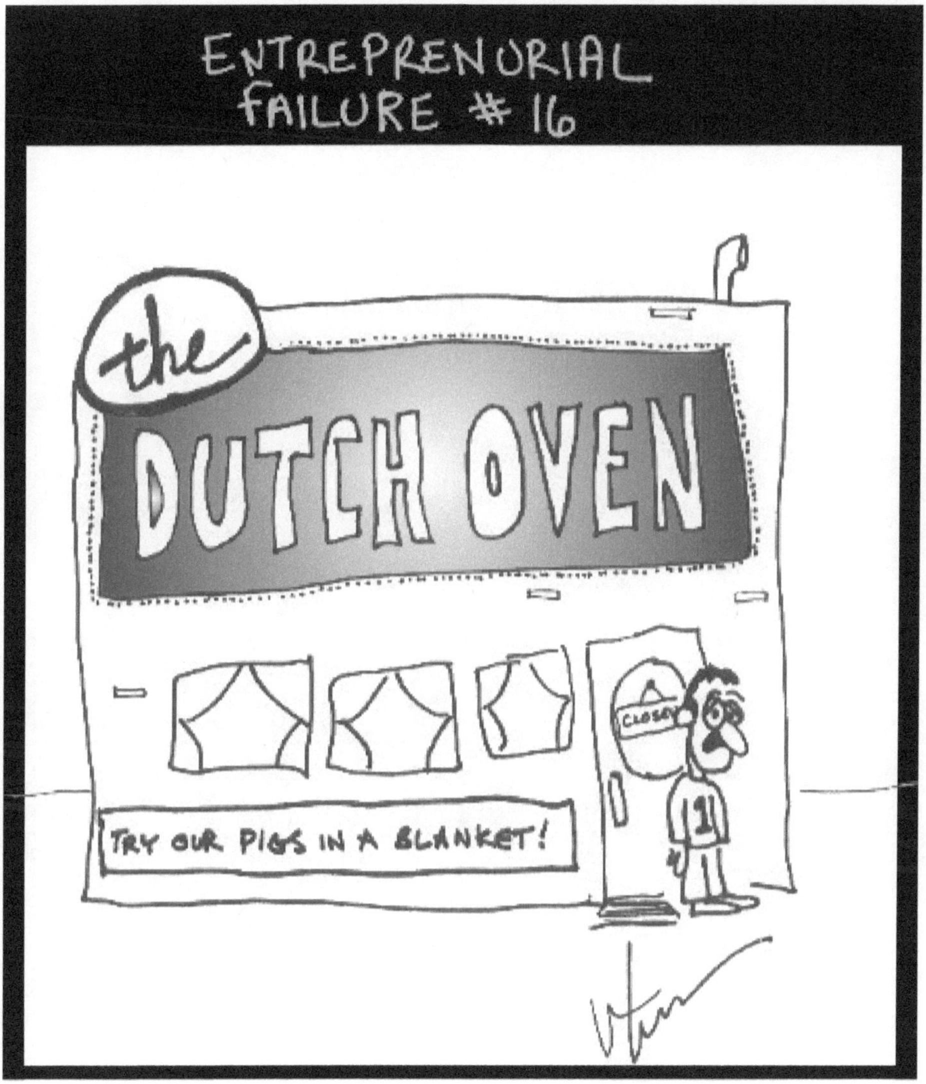
ENTREPRENURIAL FAILURE #16
the
DUTCH OVEN
CLOSED
TRY OUR PIGS IN A BLANKET!

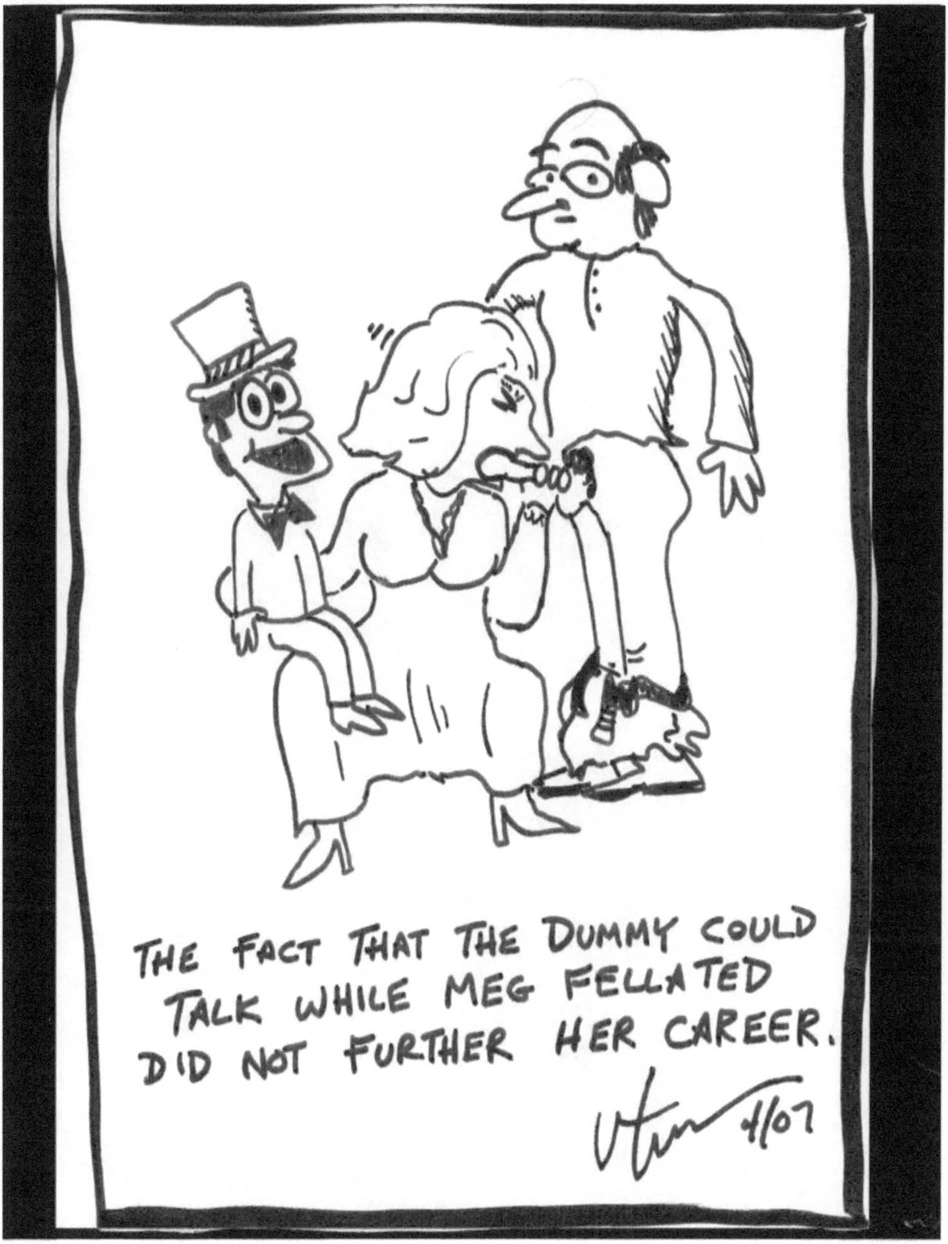
THE FACT THAT THE DUMMY COULD TALK WHILE MEG FELLATED DID NOT FURTHER HER CAREER.

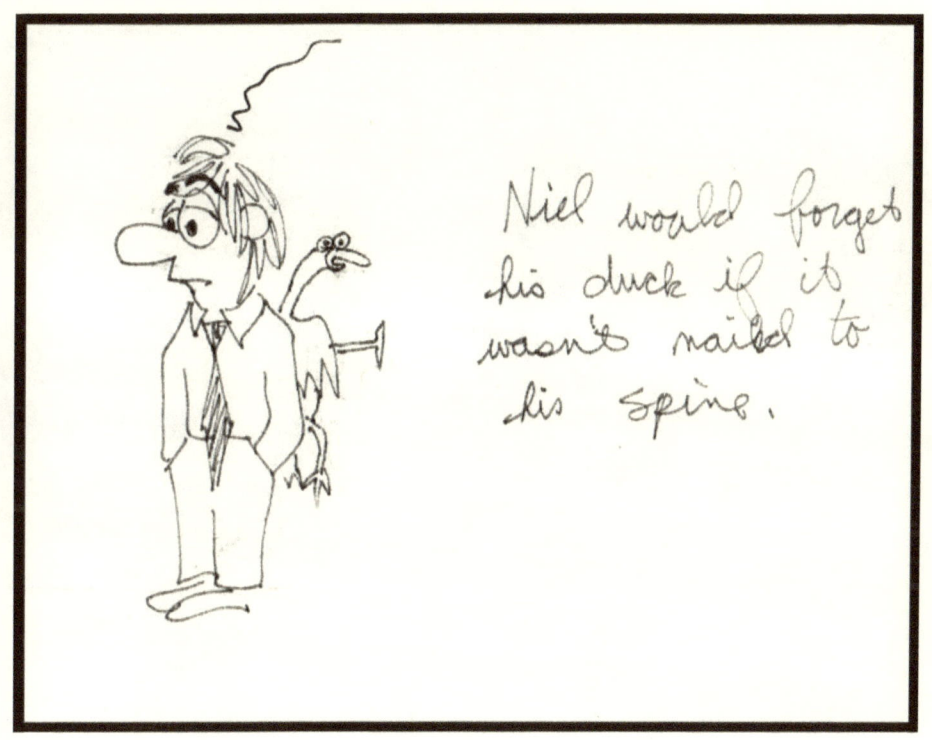

Niel would forget his duck if it wasn't nailed to his spine.

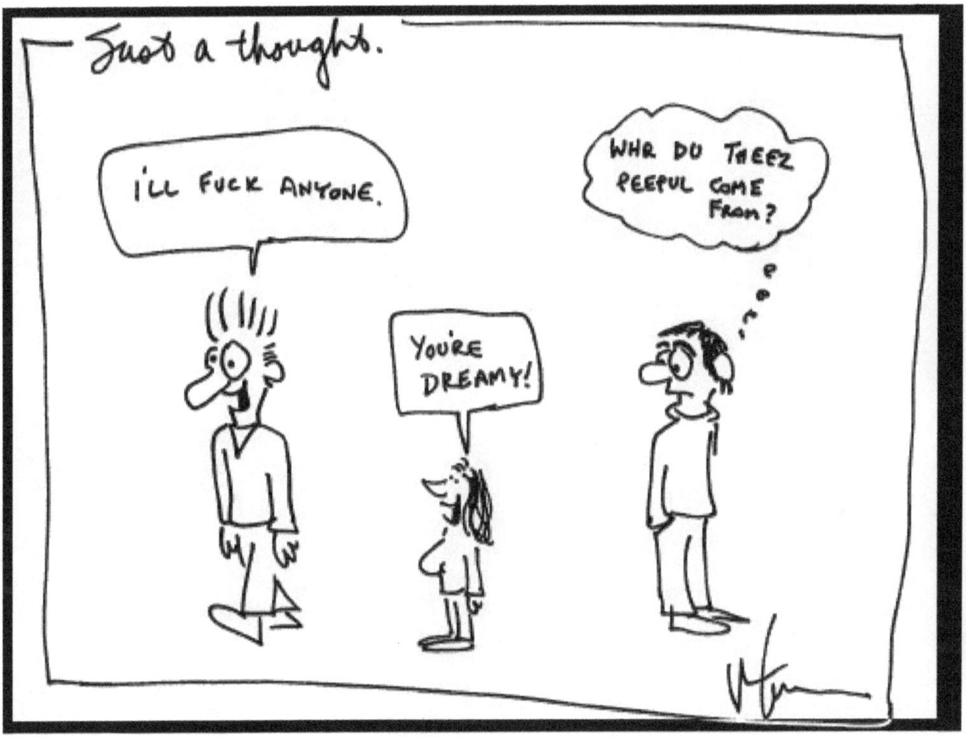
Just a thought.
I'LL FUCK ANYONE.
YOU'RE DREAMY!
WHR DU THEEZ PEEPUL COME FROM?

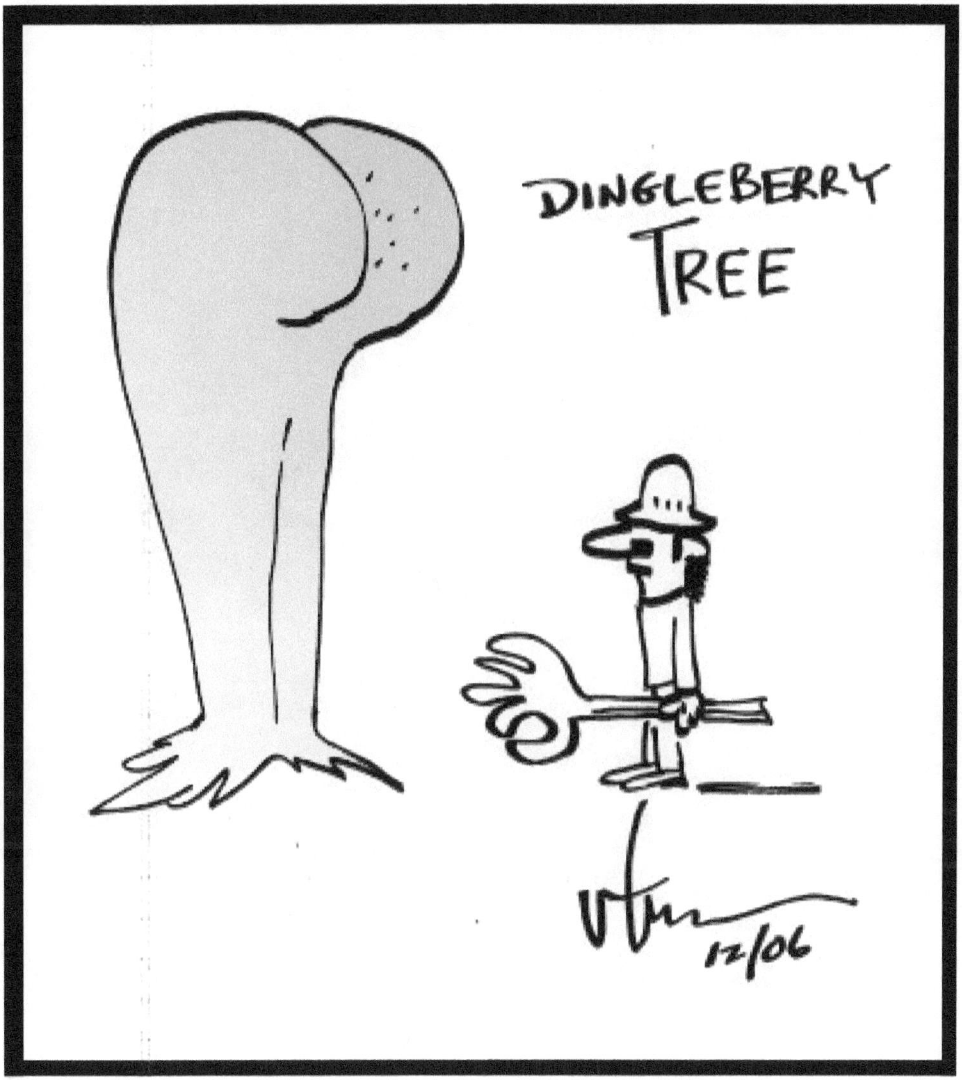
DINGLEBERRY
TREE
12/06

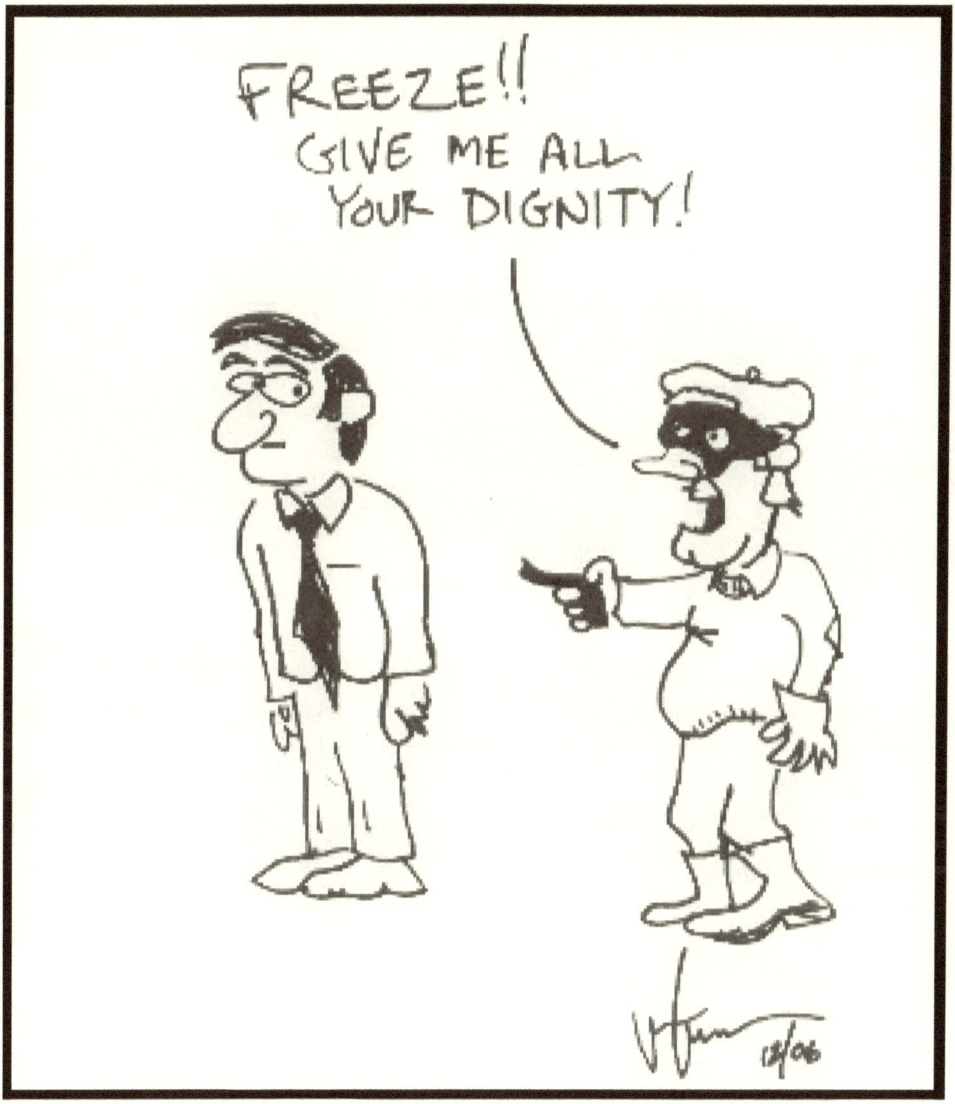
FREEZE!! GIVE ME ALL YOUR DIGNITY!

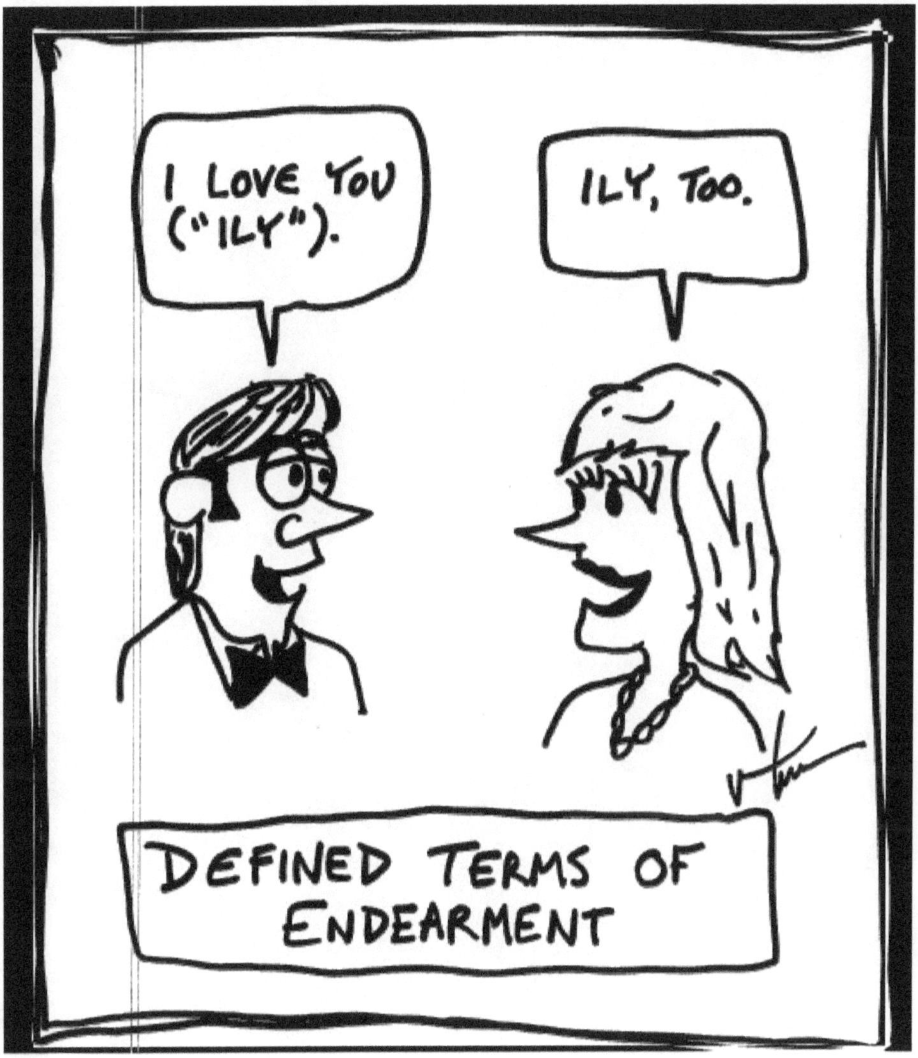
I LOVE YOU ("ILY").
ILY, TOO.
DEFINED TERMS OF ENDEARMENT

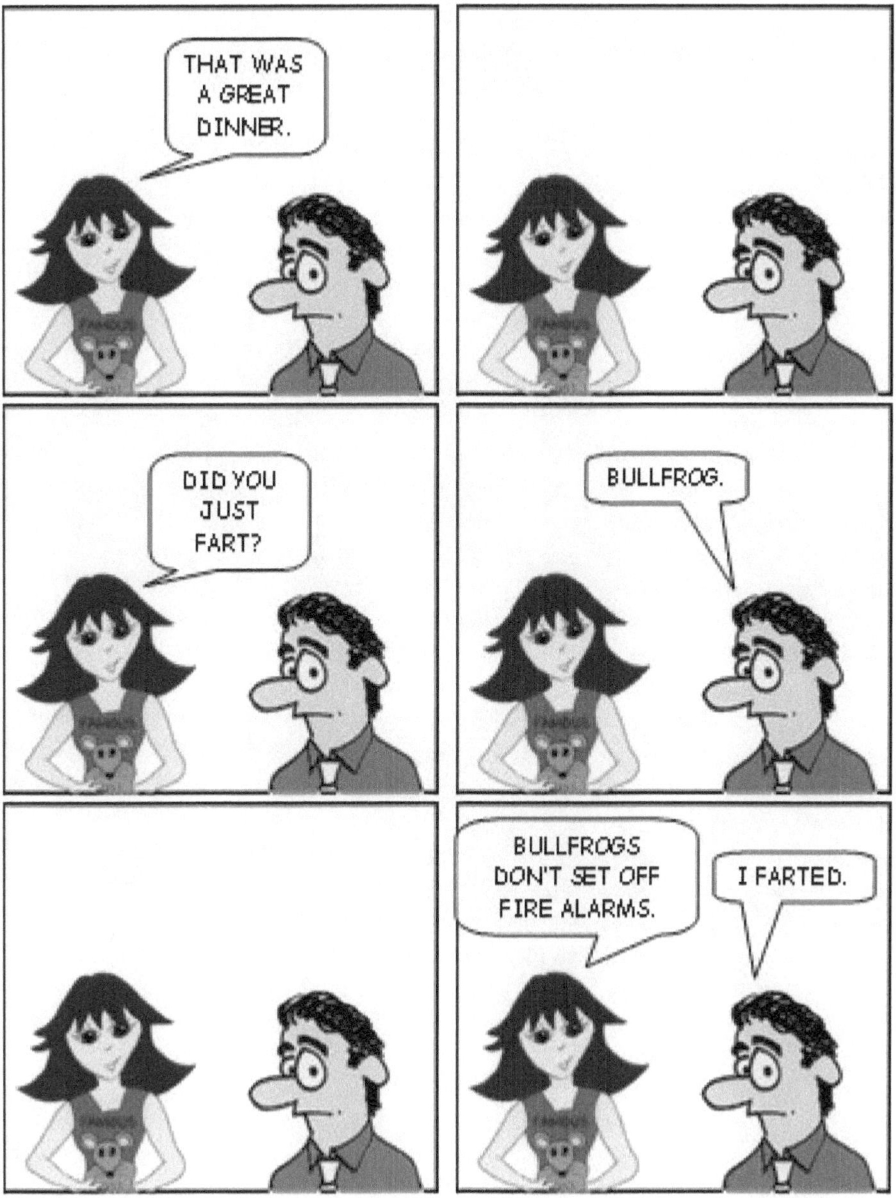
THAT WAS A GREAT DINNER.
DID YOU JUST FART?
BULLFROG.
BULLFROGS DON'T SET OFF FIRE ALARMS.
I FARTED.

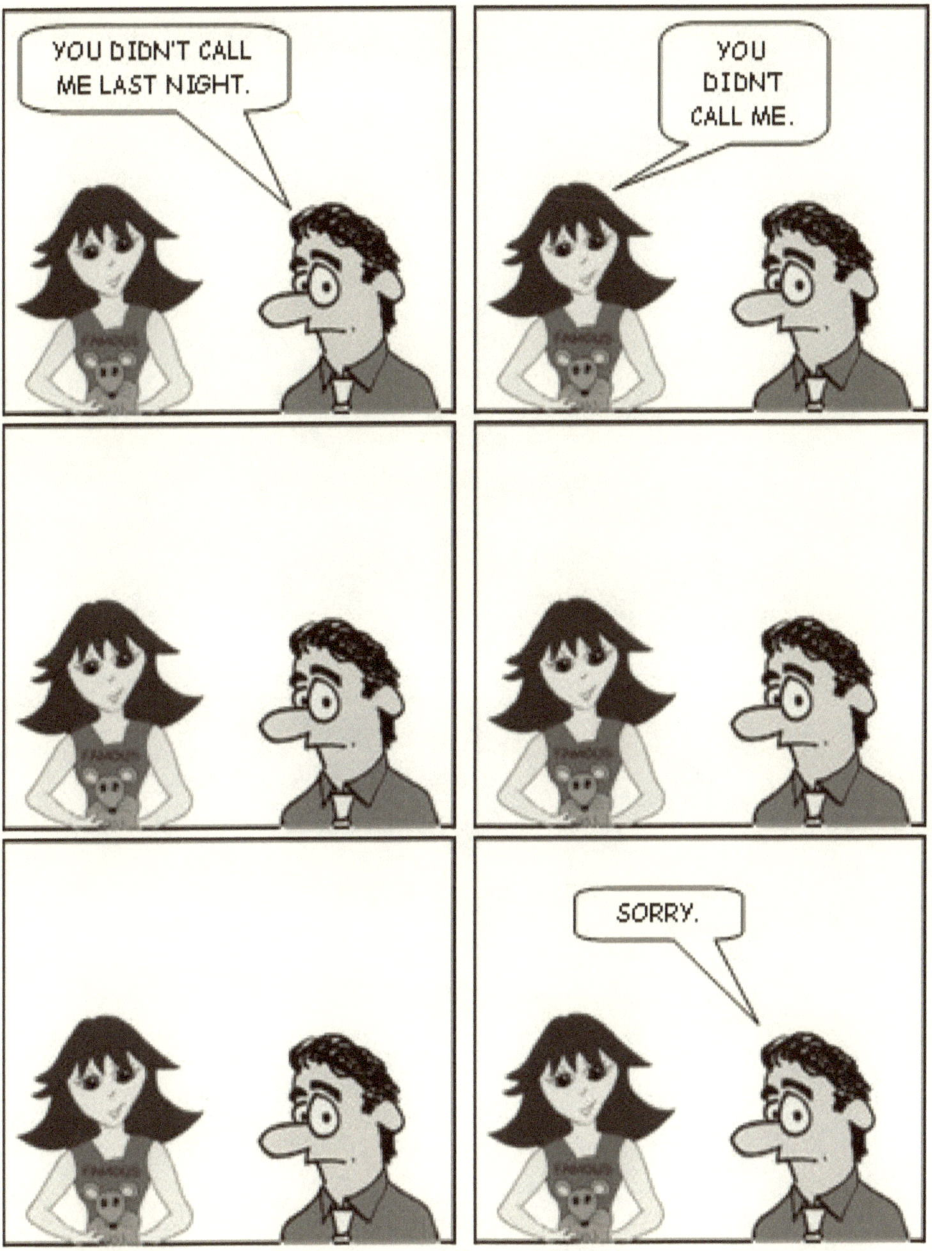
YOU DIDN'T CALL ME LAST NIGHT.
YOU DIDN'T CALL ME.
SORRY.

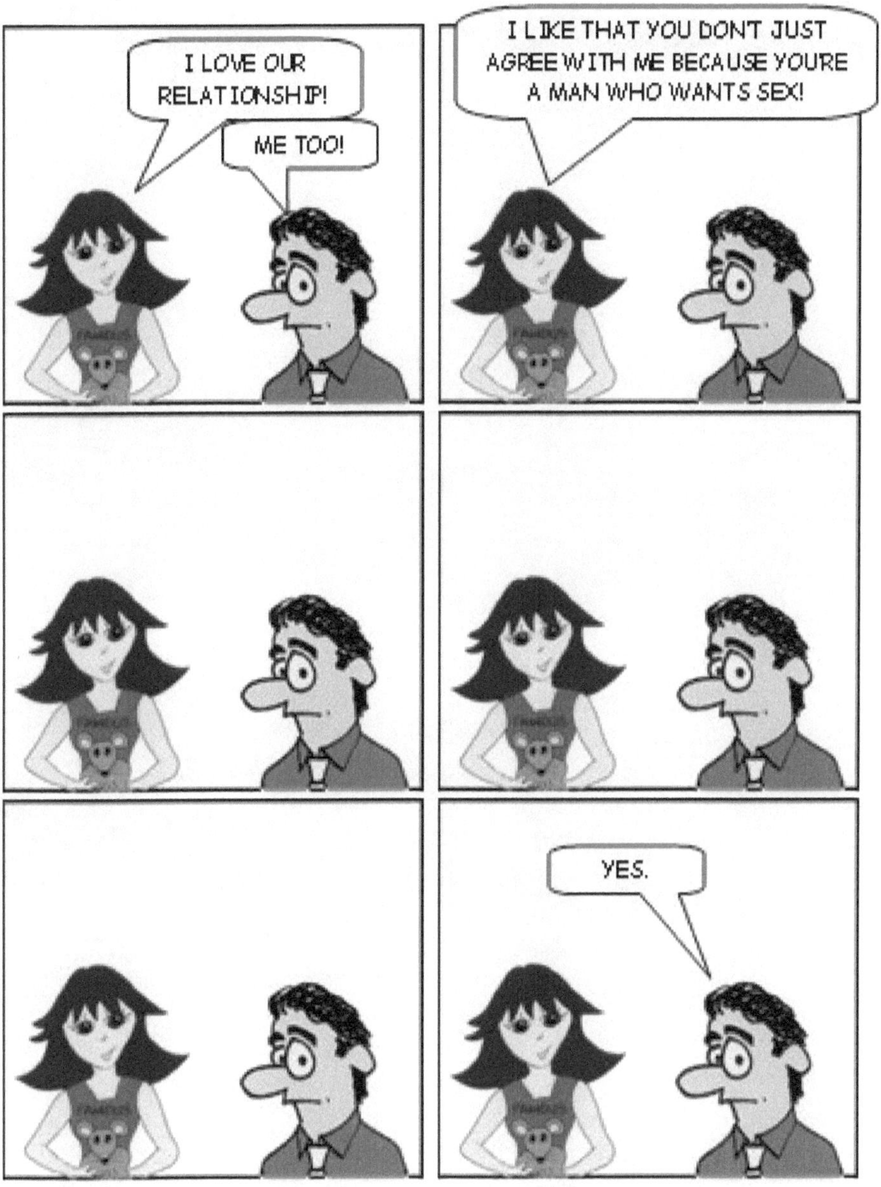
I LOVE OUR RELATIONSHIP!
ME TOO!
I LIKE THAT YOU DON'T JUST AGREE WITH ME BECAUSE YOU'RE A MAN WHO WANTS SEX!
YES.

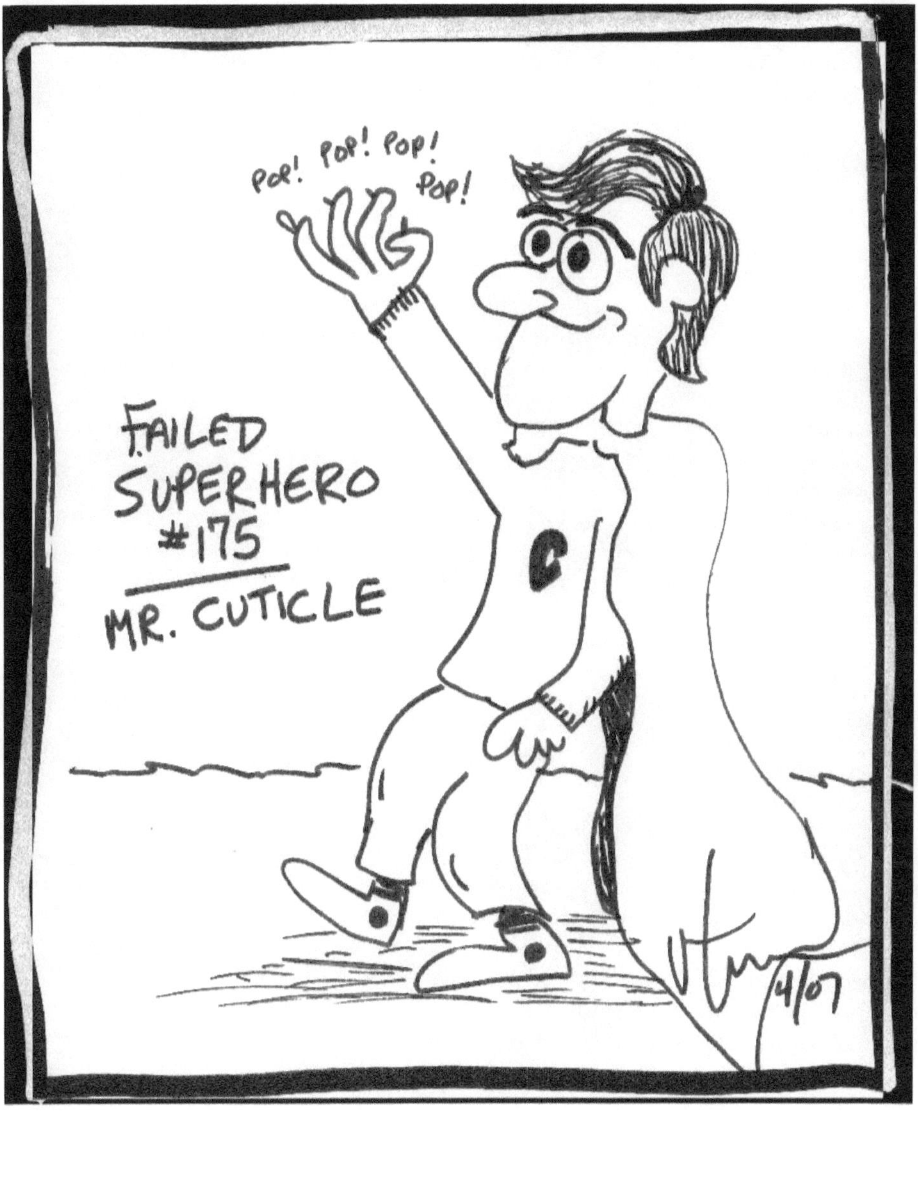
POP! POP! POP!
POP!
FAILED
SUPERHERO
#175
MR. CUTICLE
4/07

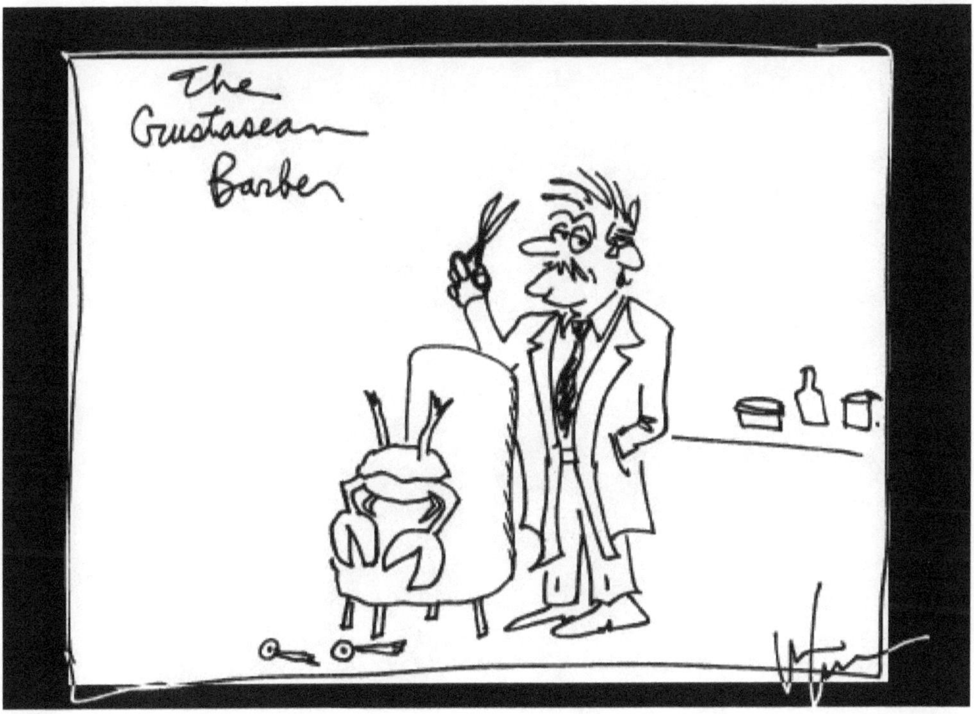
The
Crustacean
Barber

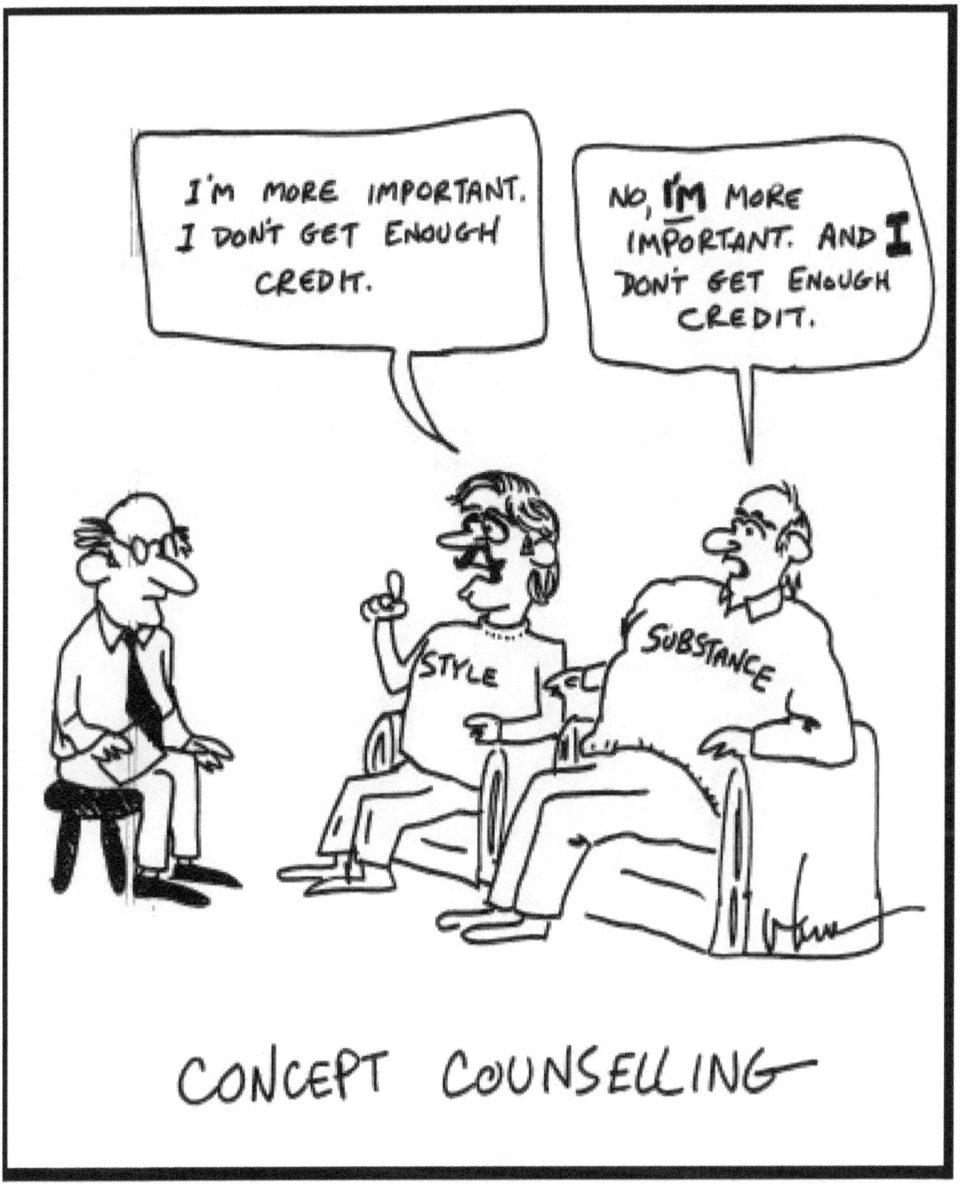
I'M MORE IMPORTANT. I DON'T GET ENOUGH CREDIT.
NO, I'M MORE IMPORTANT. AND I DON'T GET ENOUGH CREDIT.
STYLE
SUBSTANCE

CONCEPT COUNSELLING

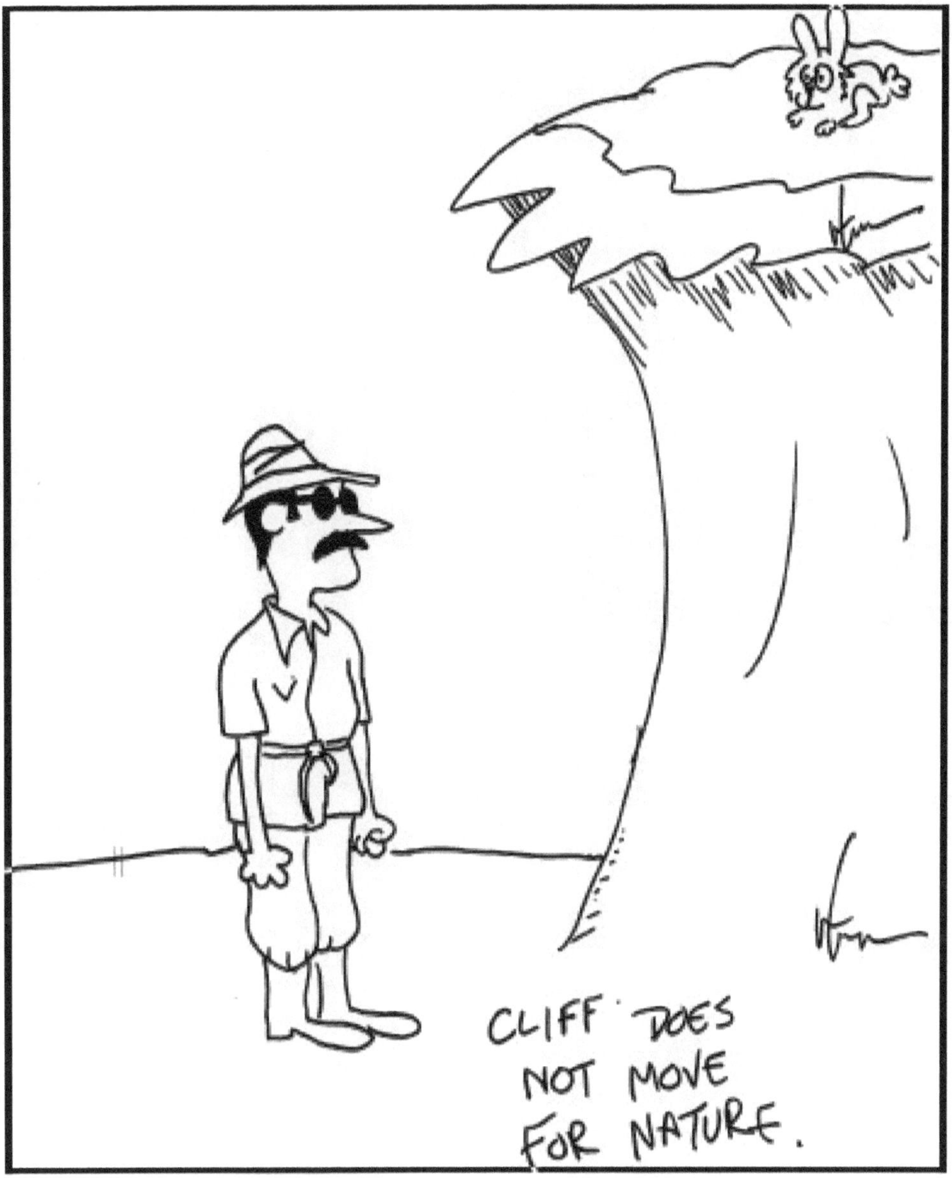
CLIFF DOES NOT MOVE FOR NATURE.

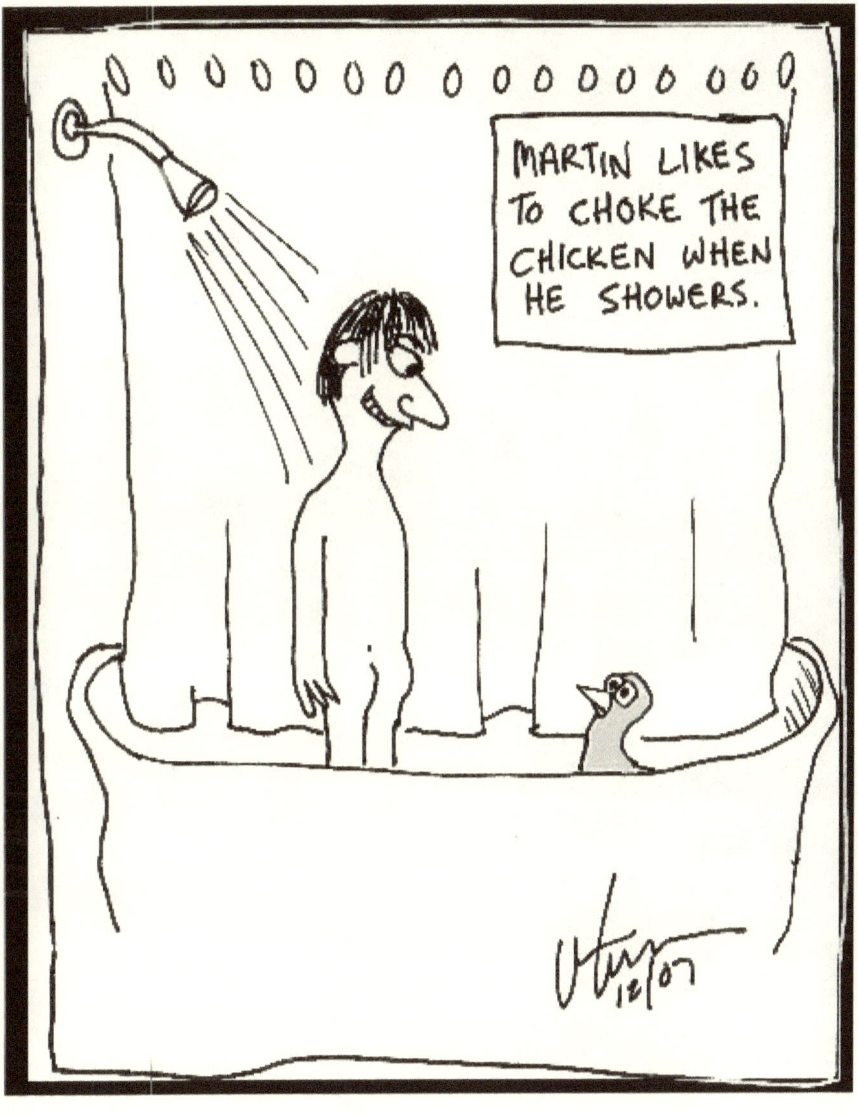
MARTIN LIKES TO CHOKE THE CHICKEN WHEN HE SHOWERS.

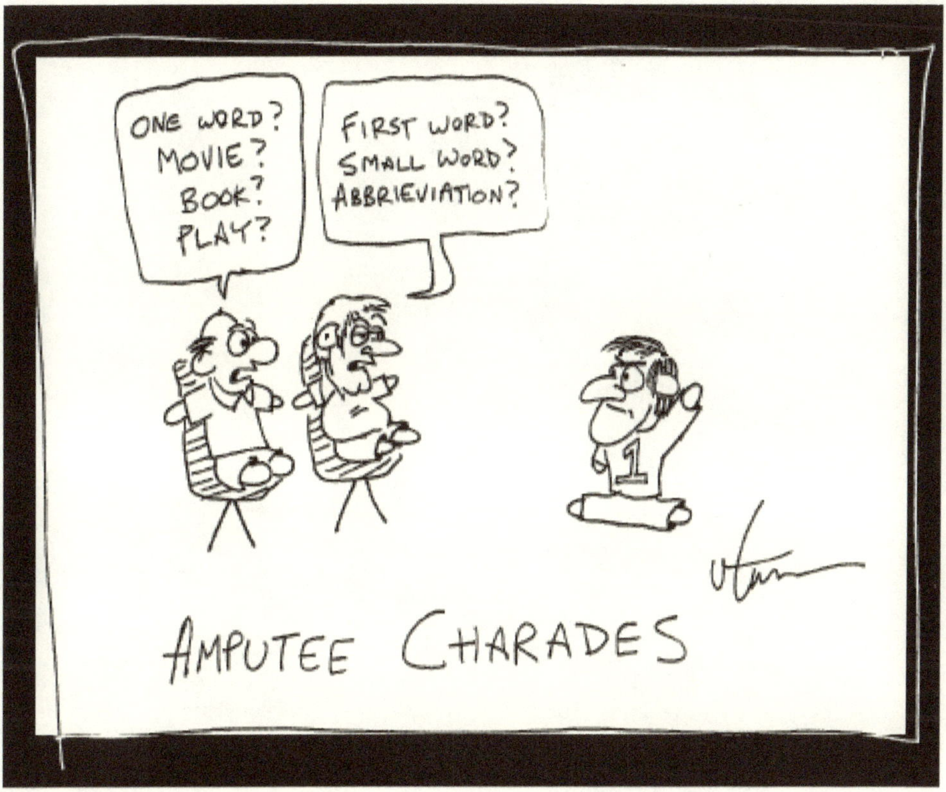
ONE WORD?
MOVIE?
BOOK?
PLAY?
FIRST WORD?
SMALL WORD?
ABBRIEVIATION?
1
AMPUTEE CHARADES

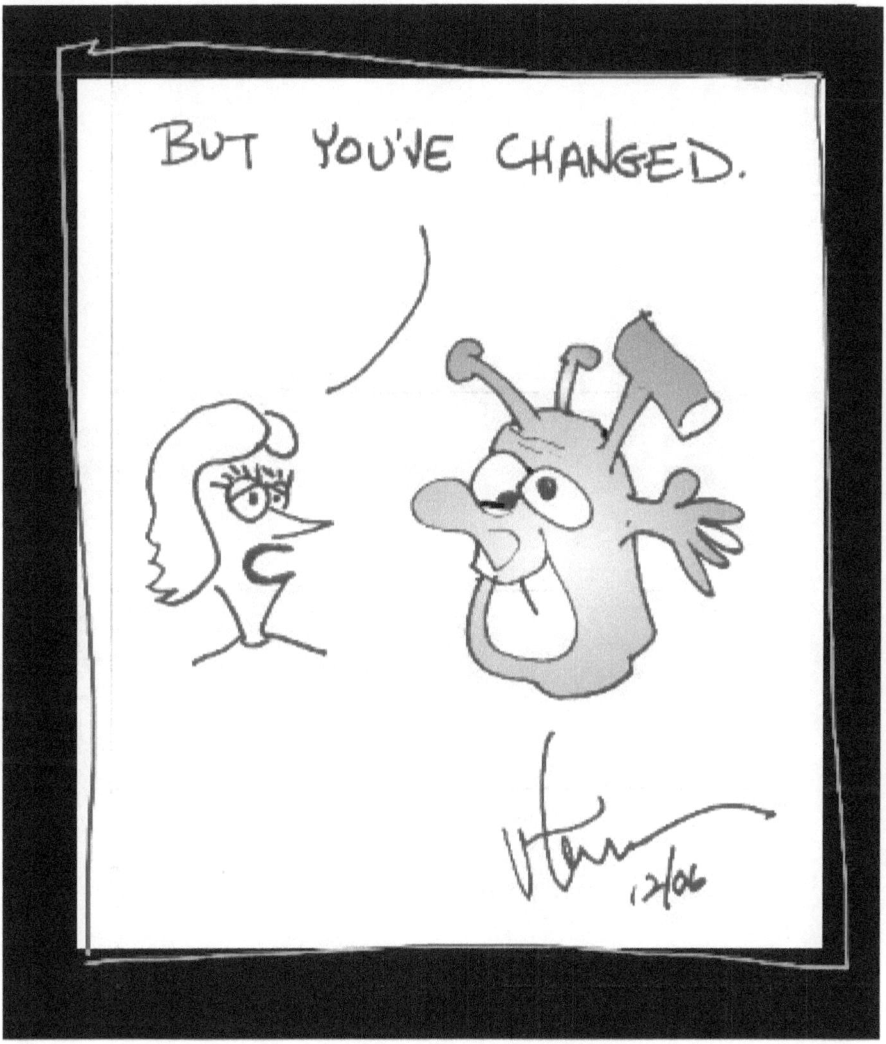
BUT YOU'VE CHANGED.
12/06

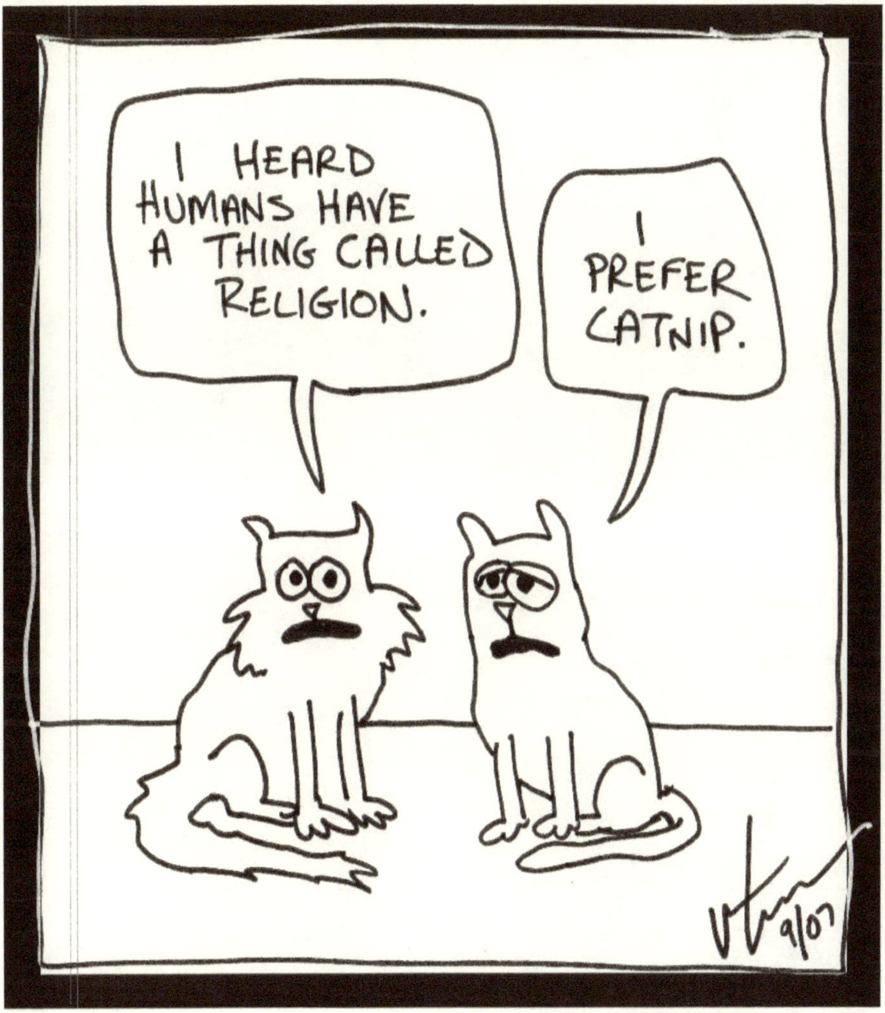
I HEARD HUMANS HAVE A THING CALLED RELIGION.
I PREFER CATNIP.

New Names For Catalogues

Old Name	New Name
Newport News	Blend In Anywhere!
Eddie Bauer	White Folk Wear
Ann Taylor	You Ugly! Buy Our Stuff!
Petsmart	More For Your Amusement Than Your Pet's
The Sharper Image	Shiny Metal Things
Lands Ends	Stuff the Color of Dirt
Harry Carter	Goofy Shit
Victoria's Secret	Big Titted Models: Miffed
Venus	Big Titted Models: Giddy
Frederick's	Big Titted Models: Constipated
Chadwicks	Big Titted Models: Distracted

9/8/05

175

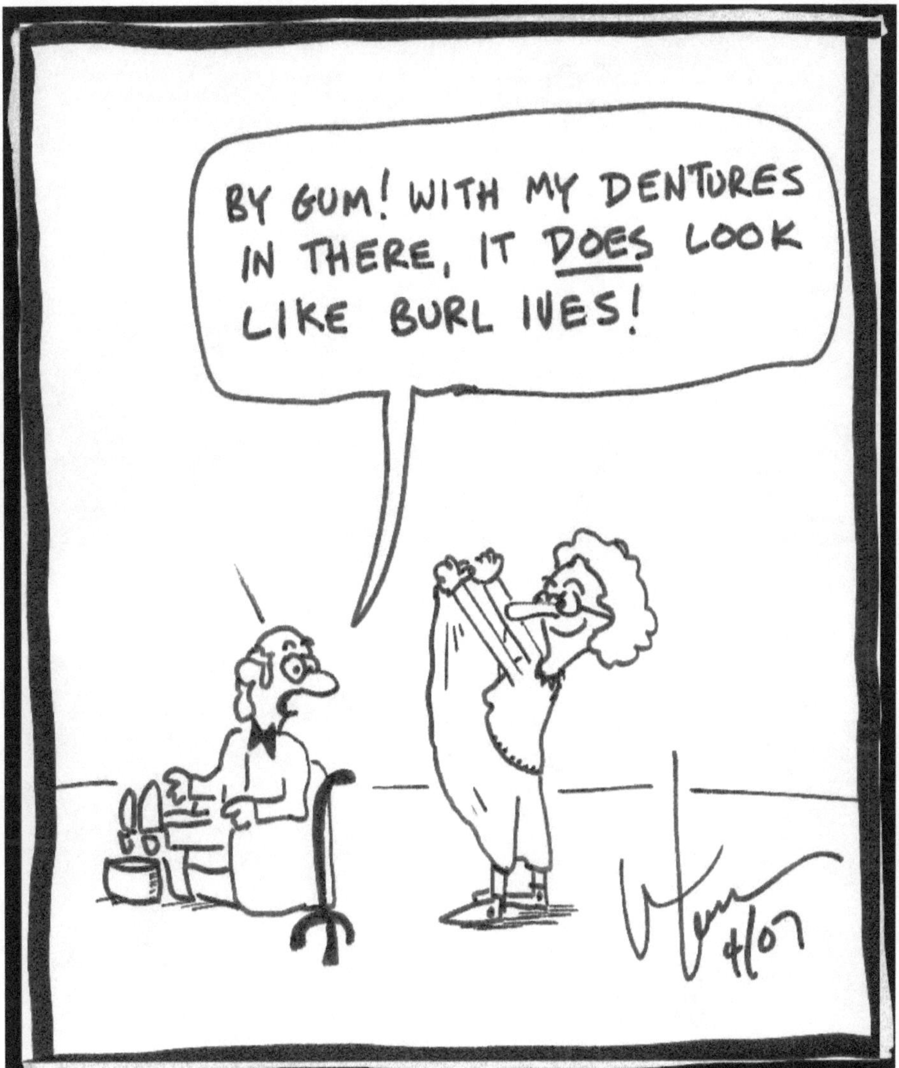
BY GUM! WITH MY DENTURES IN THERE, IT DOES LOOK LIKE BURL IVES!

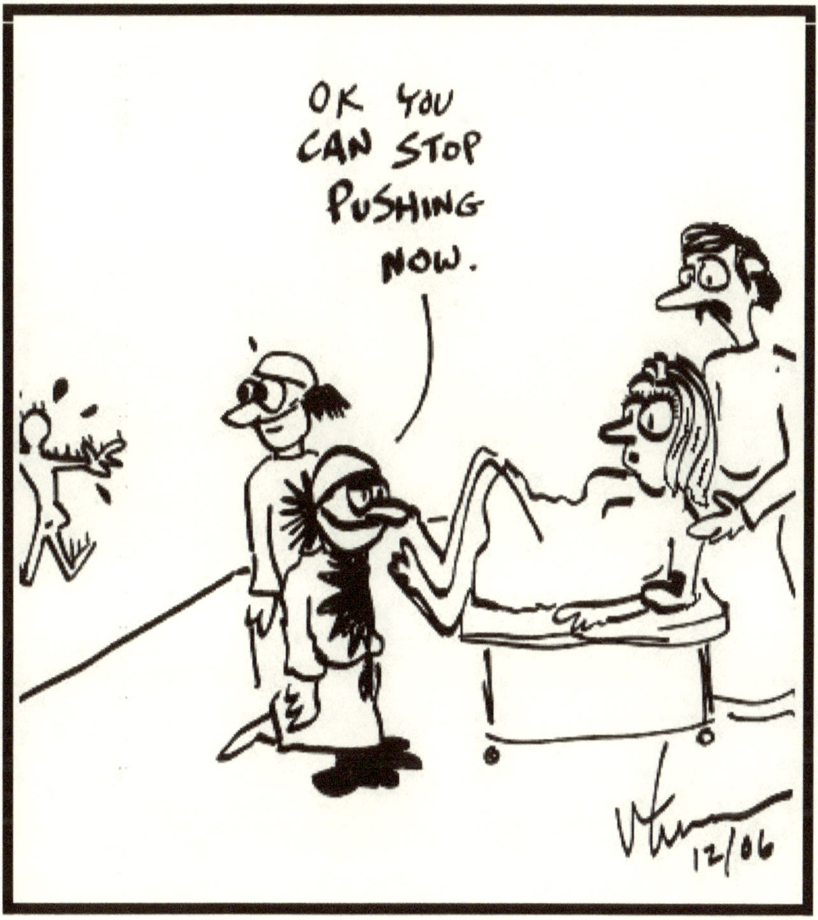
OK YOU CAN STOP PUSHING NOW.
12/06

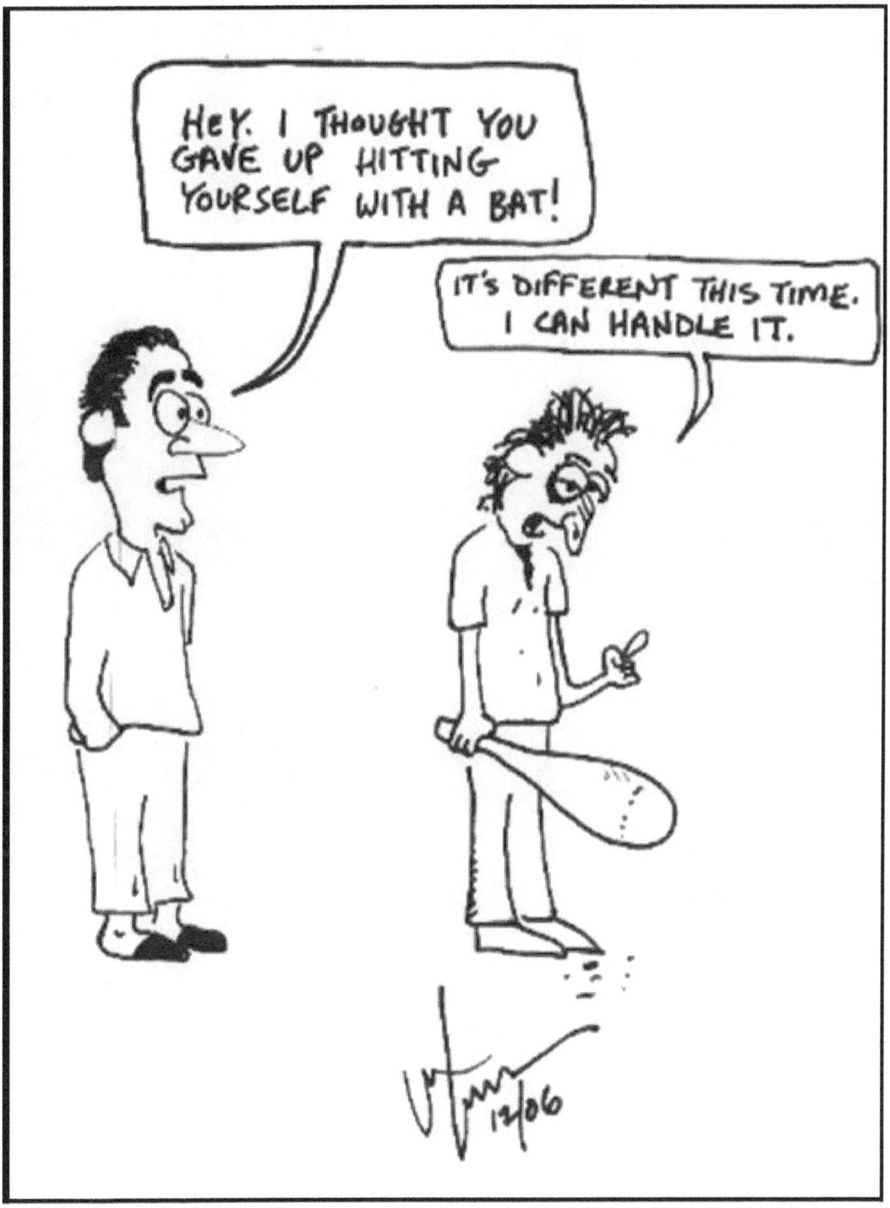
HEY. I THOUGHT YOU GAVE UP HITTING YOURSELF WITH A BAT!
IT'S DIFFERENT THIS TIME. I CAN HANDLE IT.
12/06

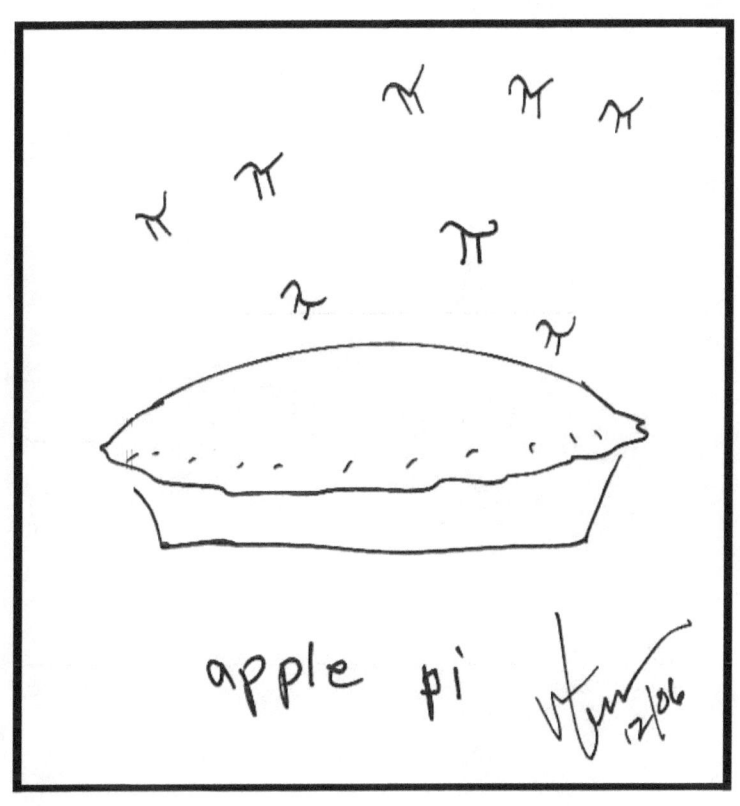

apple pi

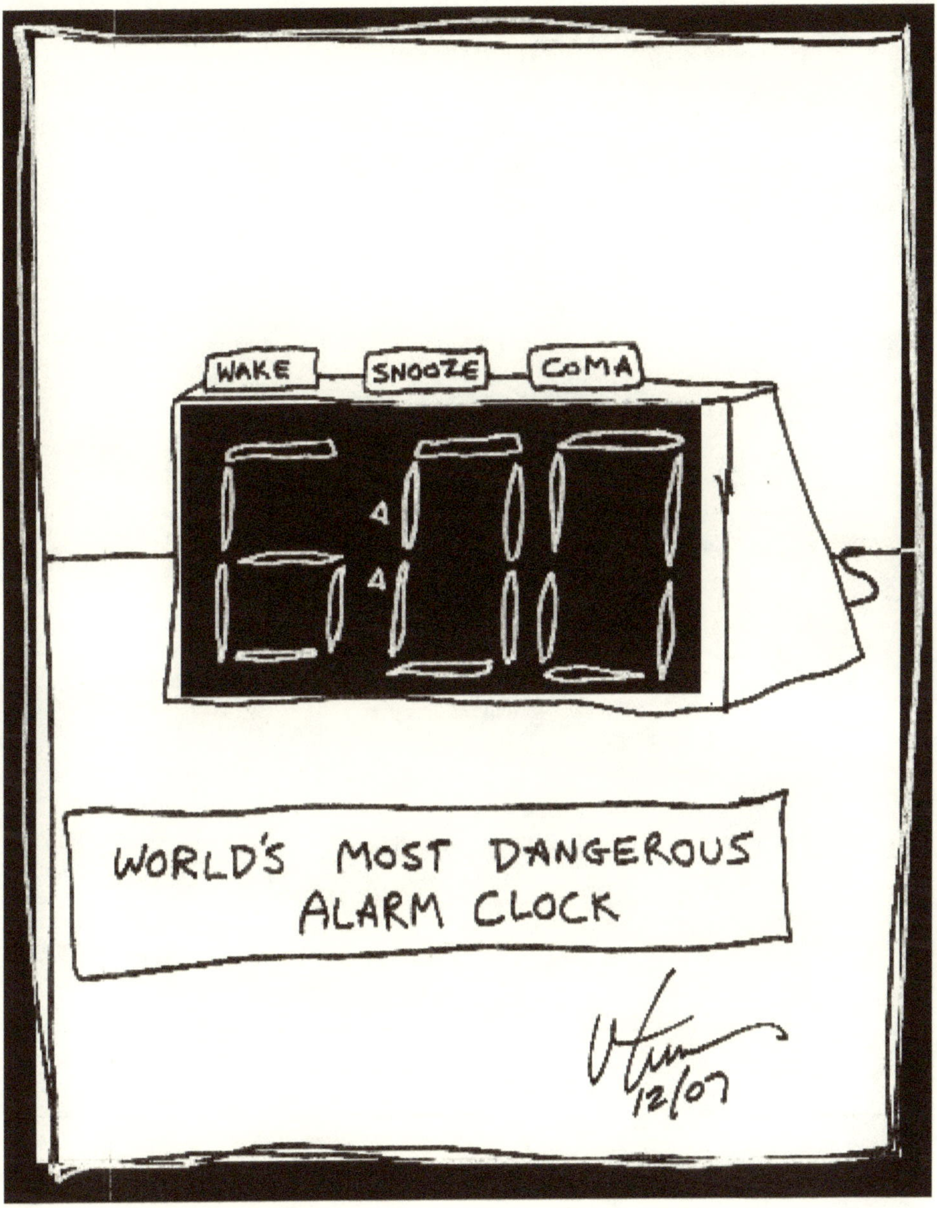
WAKE
SNOOZE
COMA
WORLD'S MOST DANGEROUS ALARM CLOCK
12/07

1975: How Fun Happened	2005: How I Make Fun Happen
Sandbox	Bar
Army Guys	Being Liberal
Guy Friends	Girlfriend
Running Around	Sitting
School	Bar
Dogs	Cats
Cartooning	Cartooning
Jumproping	Being a feminist
Club House	Bar
Cake Batter	Sushi
Talking	Chatting
Farting	Farting
Smoking a cigarette	Smoking A Pack
Riding a bike	Burning A CD
Lemonade	Bacardi Raz
All music	My Music
Walking in the Woods To Talk To Myself	Riding an Elevator To Talk to Myself
Rubbing on Stuff	Masturbation
Religion	Avoiding Religion
Atari	"Diablo II"
Seeking Acceptance	Seeking Acceptance
Everything Else	Sex

187

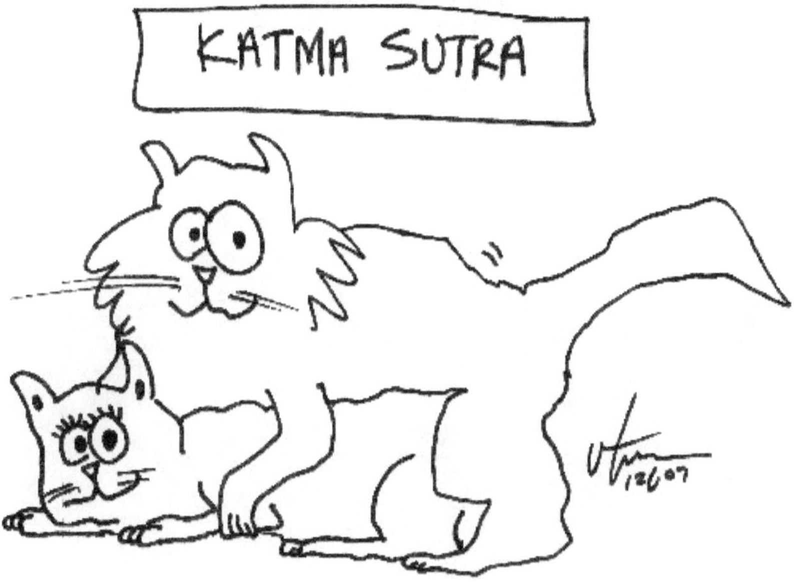
KATMA SUTRA

#15: CHURNING CATNIP

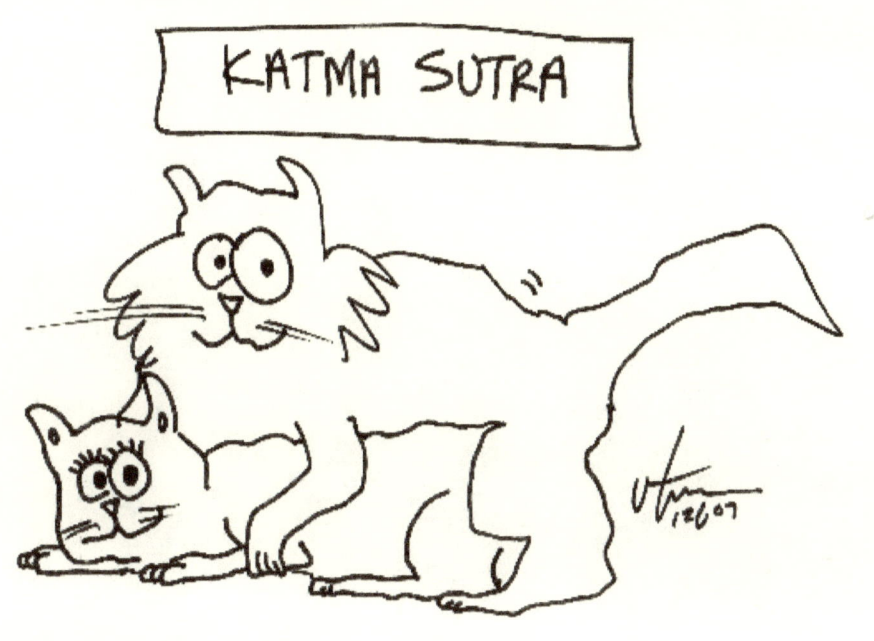

KATMA SUTRA

#32: BITING THE RADISH

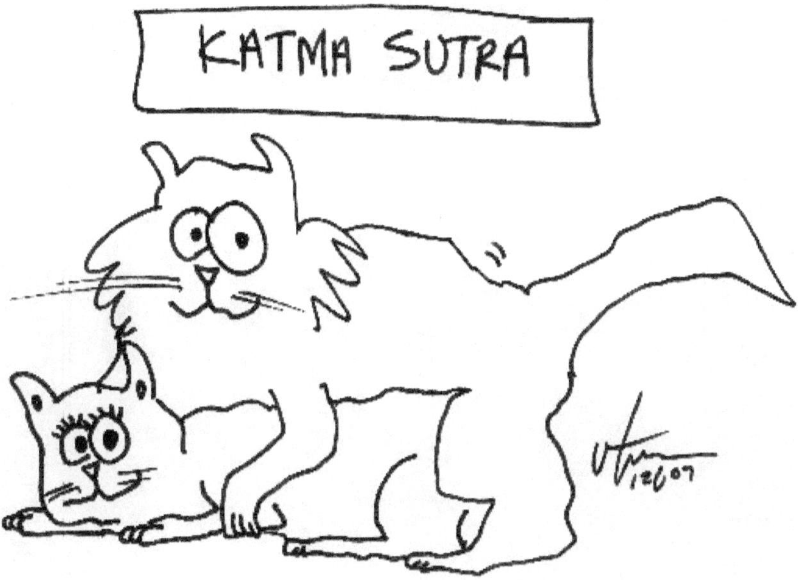
KATMA SUTRA

#41: THE SLIPPERY WALLPAPER

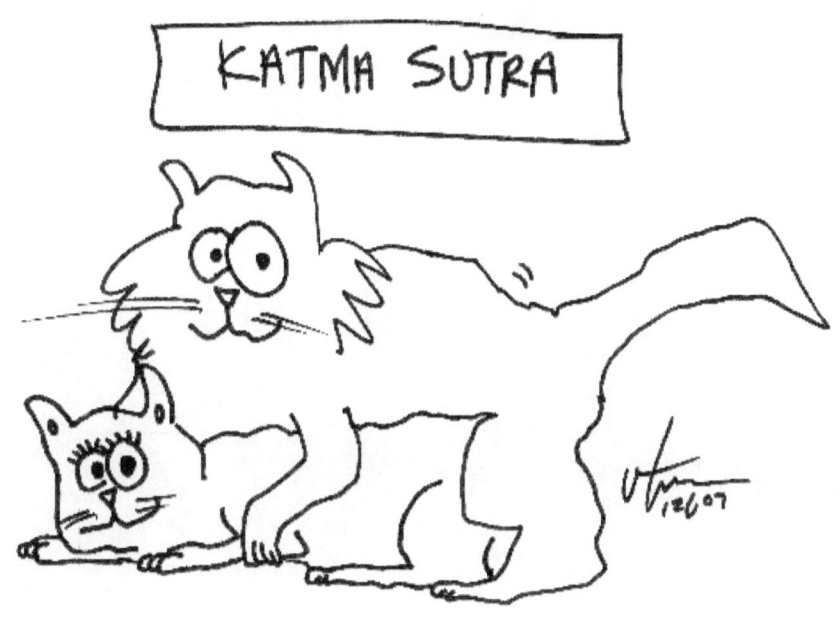

KATMA SUTRA

#53: THE ELTON JOHN

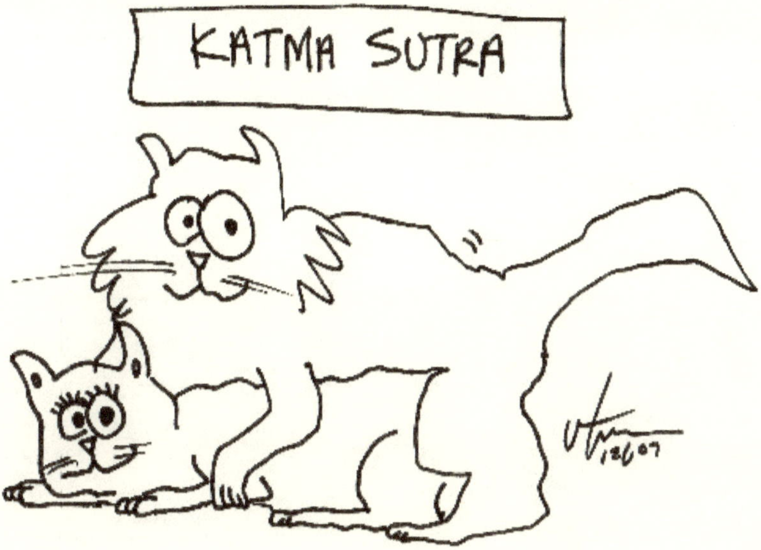
KATMA SUTRA

#67: SCRUBBING THE BUBBLE

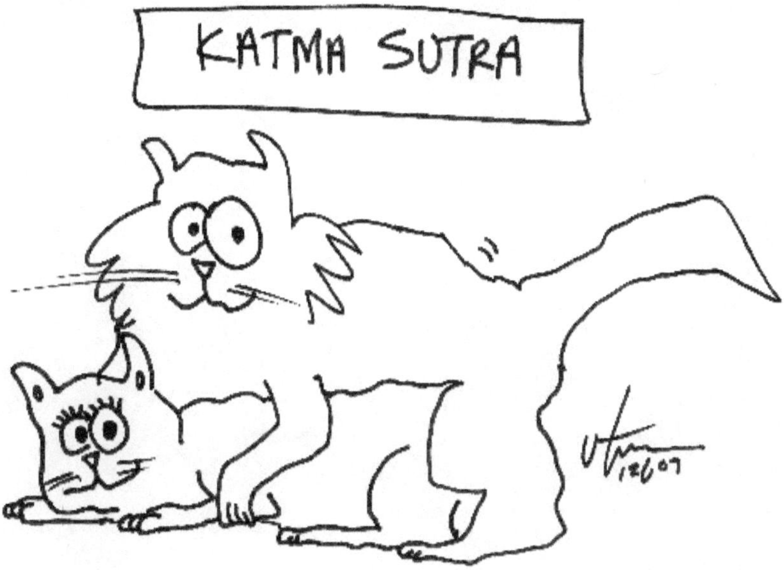
KATMA SUTRA

#74: BOILING CARROT

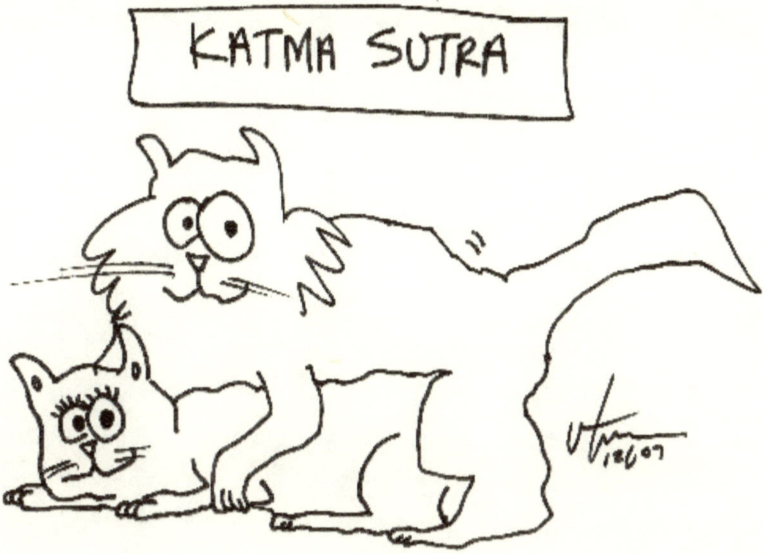
KATMA SUTRA

#80: HOLOCAUST NEVER HAPPENED

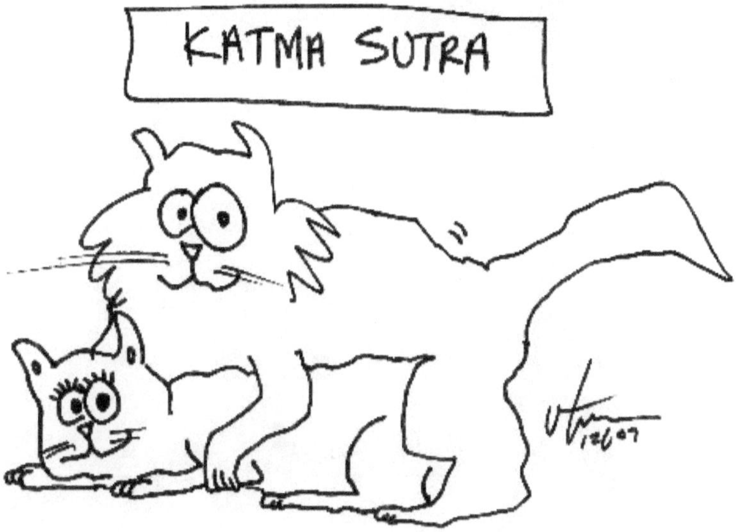
KATMA SUTRA

#95: STORMING THE CASTLE

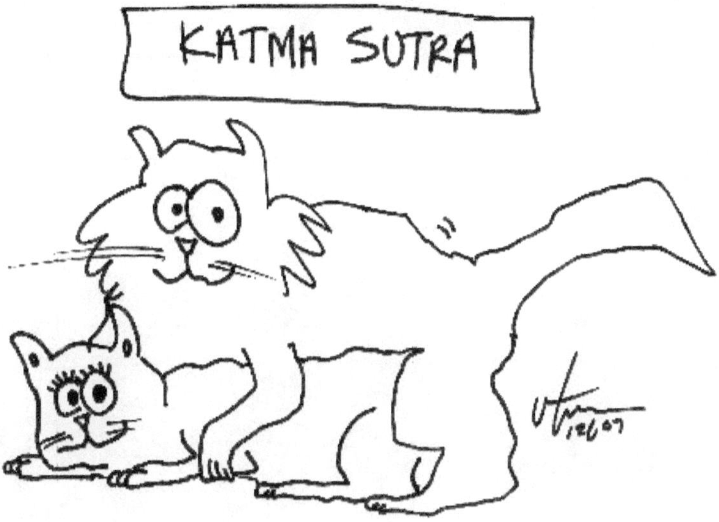
KATMA SUTRA

#102: SAVE ALL CHANGES

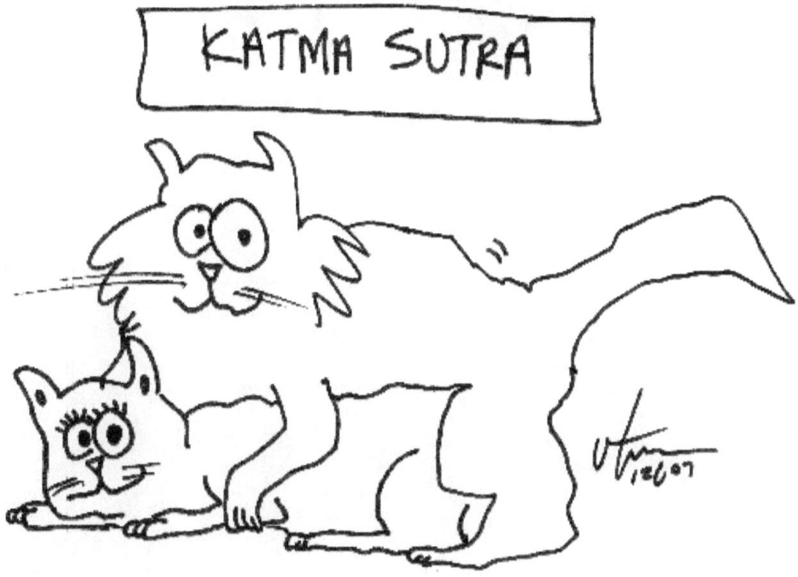
KATMA SUTRA

#114: HAIRBALL

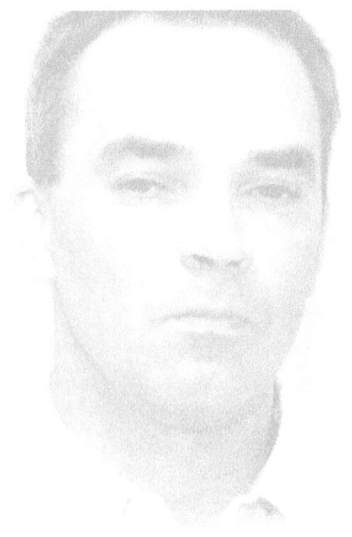

Vincent Truman is a author, director and actor in Chicago. In addition to founding the sketch comedy group Suspicious Clowns in 2001, Truman has written and appeared in the three-act play "Remote" and been published in numerous literary compilations.

He was born as the third of two children in Morris, Illinois. He currently lives in limbo with his pet peeves.

This page intentionally left blank.

www.ingramcontent.com/pod-product-compliance
Lightning Source LLC
Chambersburg PA
CBHW030003190526
45157CB00014B/404